A Light in the Darkness

Swamini Krishnamrita Prana

Mata Amritanandamayi Center
San Ramon, California, United States

A Light in the Darkness
by Swamini Krishnamrita Prana

Published by:
Mata Amritanandamayi Center
P.O. Box 613
San Ramon, CA 94583
United States
www.amma.org

First edition: October 2017

In India:
www.amritapuri.org
inform@amritapuri.org

In USA:
amma.org

In Europe:
www.amma-europe.org

Put your empty hands in mine.
Show me all the scars you hide.
And if your wings are broken
Please take mine, so yours can open too.
I'm going to stand by you.

Tears make kaleidoscopes in your eyes,
I know you're hurting, and so am I.
Love, if your wings are broken
You can borrow mine, so yours can open too.
I'm going to stand by you.

You are all I never knew I needed.
The heart, sometimes it's painful as it's beating.
And if your wings are broken
We can brave through those emotions too,
Because, I'm going to stand by you.

I guess truth is what you believe in,
I think faith is helping for no reason.
I'll be your eyes when yours can't shine,
I'll be your arms when you can't rise,
I will always stand by you...

Even if we're breaking down, we can
find a way to break through.
Even if we can't find heaven, I'll
walk through hell with you.
Love, you're not alone, because I'm
going to stand with you.

Adapted from the song, *Stand by You,*
by Rachel Platten

Introduction

*We can only dispel the darkness
by bringing in the light.*

– Amma

In today's world, it is common for people to feel lost. They battle through life without real love or authentic guidance. Far too often falsehood is presented as truth, and we find ourselves easily distracted from our dharmic (righteous) path. It is difficult to raise children to understand genuine spiritual values and principles when the world is bombarding us with so many examples to the contrary.

Amidst all of this darkness, we need a light to illumine our path, to show us the way out of suffering. Amma is that Light. She nurtures us with a mother's all-embracing love, while simultaneously disciplining us with a Guru's wise teachings.

Her life has added a whole new dimension and meaning to the word 'Amma' (mother). She has made it one of the richest and sweetest words, resounding all over the planet. Amma loves us deeply and unconditionally. She accepts us fully with all of our weaknesses and our shame. Like a cool breeze, She revives us in the parched desert of worldly existence and brings fulfillment to our lonely lives. Amma is the essence of everything beautiful, comforting and precious.

It is impossible to fully understand the magnificence of Amma; ultimately, our mind cannot grasp who She truly is. But it is easy to see Her greatest miracle: the ability to transform our hearts. She takes ordinary, worldly people, and turns us into something good – into people who want to give our lives in service. She has done this for thousands of people from all walks of life.

Transformation is a slow process, one that can only be achieved with infinite patience, and yet, one day each of us will blossom. A devotee recently reminded me of this with an amazing story. It unfolded a few years back when Amma visited this lady's house at the end of an Australian tour.

She had an old cactus plant (in a slightly broken pot) sitting by the front door of her home. It had never flowered or changed appearance over the many years it had been there. The family had virtually forgotten about its existence, but as Amma was about to enter the house, She bent down and reverently caressed the cactus plant with great gentleness.

The lady of the house felt a little ashamed. She was embarrassed that she had not hidden it away and placed a grander looking plant in its place, but in the excitement of Amma's visit, she had forgotten to move it.

After Amma had blessed their house, the family followed Her to the airport. When they returned home a few hours after saying goodbye, they were shocked and amazed at the miracle they beheld. The lowly cactus plant, in its broken pot, had taken on a burst of glory. It was now wearing a majestic crown of cactus flowers. Blushing in its newfound state of consecration, it flowered.

The family was completely stunned that their boring old cactus plant had been miraculously transformed by a simple touch from Amma. The very next day, it was proudly enshrined in a new pot and given a place of pride in a sunny spot near the family altar.

Often we may seem a lot like that prickly, old cactus plant. We can remain in a static state of cantankerous and irritable non-growth for very long periods of time. Although we receive so many blessings, we stubbornly refuse to change (sometimes prickly cactus plants have even more surrender than we do). Luckily, Amma never gives up on us. Miracles of growth and transformation take place wherever She goes.

This book chronicles the stories of 18 different people – 18 lives that Amma has transformed, one heart at a time. Each story is unique, and each one is a testament to Amma's true glory, as She brings one person after another out of their pain and into the light.

Not everyone has come from as deep or as dark a place as some of the people in these stories – but there certainly are those who have – and thanks to Amma, there are now thousands of stories of healing and transformation happening all over the world. For now, let's start with chronicling just 18.

Amma is teaching us, day by day, to forget a little bit about ourselves and to think about giving to others instead. Slowly, with immeasurable patience and boundless love, Amma is showing us, through Her own example, how to blossom and become shining lights in the darkness.

Chapter 1

Learning to Serve

In a gentle way, you can shake the world.

– Mahatma Gandhi

When I was 20 years old I fell in love with God. Our love only lasted one summer, but it was a passionate affair full of joy and light. Every time I sang in prayer, I was overwhelmed with pure rapture. The world was a beautiful place, full of life and colour. God was magnificent, ever-present and devastatingly glorious.

At the end of that summer, I left my privileged life in the West and started to travel, visiting some of the poorest countries in the world.

I first went to Africa. My friends and I camped out at Ngorogoro Crater, the most breathtaking place I had ever seen. As the sun set bright colours ripped across the sky, painting the most magnificent portrait of God. My heart danced in ecstasy

11

at the sight. The moon rose, the fire died, and we all drifted to sleep.

That night our campsite was violently attacked by a rabid hyena. A newlywed woman was bitten. She died three weeks later. Shortly thereafter, a good friend of mine was violently raped. The local authorities did nothing.

As distressing as these tragedies were, they were nothing compared to the poverty. Everywhere we went there were dirty, starving children begging in the streets with no one to look after them. People lived in houses built from scraps of trash.

I was experiencing the sorrow of the world for the first time – and I felt utterly betrayed by my Beloved.

I moved from city to city and country to country in search of a way to heal my heart. Every time I moved I experienced temporary joy and excitement. When the misery returned, I would move again in search of a new adventure.

Over the next six years I lived in thirteen different cities, in seven different countries on four different continents. I witnessed oppression, terrorism, civil war and violence. Love became a fantasy, lost in a savage world.

My heart slammed shut.

Clearly God didn't care, so neither would I. When I heard people praying, I would close the door to my room and cry.

The afternoon before I met Amma, I remember feeling completely hopeless and alone. I was secure in my belief that love was nothing more than lust and that God was mentally sick. The world was just too full of pain.

I had spent the whole day, and the day before, watching violent TV re-runs and waiting until I could quit my job and move someplace else. I was suffering from mild depression and terrible anxiety.

Amma changed everything.

My friends only got me into the car that night by bribing me with promises of "really good chai." I was willing to go, but I made it clear: I was only in this for the chai. I spent the entire car ride trying to set them straight, "This Amma thing is idol worship," I argued. They just rolled their eyes and reminded me about the chai.

Then She walked into the room: a tiny, beautiful woman in a pure white sari. Her complexion was the colour of Krishna...She touched my hand. My whole hand...I still remember.

When I went for darshan that night, Amma planted a seed into my heart. I could feel it. Over the next twenty-four hours, it sprouted. The following day I was desperate to get back to Her.

I went for darshan again that night and broke down crying. I heard Amma's voice so clearly in my mind: "My darling daughter, it is not God who is twisted, it is your mind." I sat in the post-darshan area, sobbing hysterically. God was beautiful after all. I yearned to be close to Her again.

Amma kept looking at me and laughing. Every time She did this, I laughed with Her for a moment. Then the violent tears would come back again, shaking my whole body to the core. I grieved for the years I had lost in so much anger and pain. Before that darshan, I had been completely stuck and hopeless, but now She was breaking me free. She looked at me over and over again, Her eyes sparkling with joy and compassion.

Several years passed. My life transformed. Every time I saw Amma, one more layer of pain would evaporate like smoke. Layer after layer of suffering slid right off.

I visited Amma's ashram in India. When I first arrived, I remember sitting on the floor, immersed in seva and spontaneously breaking into giggles. I just could not believe that heaven existed on earth, and here I was sitting right in the middle of it.

Amma deals with the suffering of the world by serving. She has orphanages, schools and charity hospitals. She builds houses for the homeless, feeds the hungry, gives pensions to widows, and provides disaster relief all over the world...the list of Her charities goes on and on. When I encountered a world filled with suffering, I got lost in desperate grief. When Amma sees suffering, She transforms it.

While traveling on South India tour a few years ago, we stopped for some time in one of Amma's orphanages. These children had nothing, but because of Amma, they now have a future filled with hope. When She sang, they all stood up and danced in bliss.

They reached out their small hands, longing to touch Her, grasping for Her belly. She held their hands, looked deeply into their eyes and danced with them.

What I have come to realize is that the problems of life will never just evaporate. We live in a world filled with darkness and pain. Sometimes it hurts, it's true, but with Amma's grace and the proper understanding, we no longer have to choose to suffer.

When Amma holds me in Her arms, the truth becomes so clear: love is real. I hadn't known that. Before I met Amma, I had never actually experienced love. She shows me that no matter how dark the world may be, underneath it all, there is only love.

Amma gives me the strength that I need to face each day with joy and gratitude.

Thanks to Amma, everyday is a miracle.

When interviewed by journalists, Amma often talks about the suffering She witnessed as a child. She knew then that Her life was meant to uplift humanity. When Amma receives us for darshan, She helps us begin to feel our own inner nature: the 'Self', which we so seldom experience. When we meet Amma, it is as though we have been drinking only sugared soda to quench our thirst; when we come into contact with pure water, it is so refreshing for our body, mind and soul. Amma is the pure water of our true nature: our beautiful, inspiring true nature.

It has been said that in Vrindavan (Sri Krishna's birthplace), Radha only saw Sri Krishna one time, by the Yamuna River. But from that moment onwards, she always loved Him. It is like this between Amma and us. Even though we may only have darshan one time with Amma, She will never forget us; She will always love us so deeply, through all of eternity.

Chapter 2

Becoming a Star

Let the beauty you love be what you do.

– Rumi

Ever since I was in high school, I wanted to be in the theatre. I yearned for the romance, the lights, the glory, the wealth and the fame. Being up on that stage – in front of thousands of people – I wanted to be a star. I would be a beautiful, glowing star, brighter than anything else on this earth.

I remember the very first time I went to the theatre. It was electric, and I immediately knew that this was all I wanted from life.

When I was in my early twenties, I moved to California to pursue my dream. I worked in theatre companies and on production crews. I assisted directors and began climbing my way up. Shows that I worked on were beginning to win major awards.

Dreams of Broadway and Hollywood were shining brightly in my mind.

Then I got fired – and as funny as it may sound, it was the biggest blessing in my life.

There is a darker side to the theatre, the side I cringe at now, but had no choice but to participate in then. Life in the theatre is dazzling, exciting and addicting – but it also brings the clubs, the alcohol, the drugs, the fights and the one-night-stands…

The stress in that industry is tremendous, and the competition is dog-eat-dog. Everyone is constantly going for the next show, the next gig, the next promotion. It is a whirlwind of constant movement and constant auditions. If you can't cut it, you fall by the wayside, forgotten. These parties were the way to stand out and stay noticeable. It's what everybody did; there were no other options.

When a homeless man uses drugs, we call him a crack-head. When a movie star does it in the back room of an exclusive nightclub, we call her daring and exotic.

If I wanted to make connections and rub shoulders with the rich and famous, I needed to be where the action was. The parties were the only way to stay relevant, to be a part of the scene.

At these parties, my routine was always the same. I would sit in the corner and slowly sip a beer, flashing a fake wedding ring to keep the wrong people away (men and women). When a drunken woman with her clothes falling off her shoulders would approach me and ask for my phone number, I would say, "Oh no, I'm sorry, my husband is just outside."

When a sleazy man would invite me to his room, I would tell him, "I'm sorry, my girlfriend is expecting me home tonight."

The creep's reply would always be the same, "Sweetheart, no one would ever have to know…"

One night a man approached me. His pupils were the size of coins from intoxication. He kept trying to touch me. I smacked him, "Stand down, savage!" I yelled.

I was living in Sodom and Gomorrah. It was the complete opposite of anything Godly or spiritual. Everything about the industry was extravagant, wasteful, and lustful. The industry that once inspired people to dream had become a peddler of unrighteousness.

To be honest, I never wanted to participate in any of it. My childhood dream had led me down a dark path – I still desperately wanted to act, I just wished it could be different. 'There has to be something better than this,' I prayed.

Deep inside it didn't feel right – *I* didn't feel right.

Getting fired saved me. When Amma came to my city a few weeks later, for the first time I could remember, my calendar was completely free. I made my way to the program, not knowing what to expect.

I had everything I ever wanted: money, connections, the potential for fame, but the night I met Amma everything changed – *everything.* My first darshan was more blissful than the strongest drug, more thrilling than the most successful production. In that very first hug, I knew I finally found that 'special something' I had been looking for.

I can't say things changed all at once, I still struggled with myself. I knew the life I was leading left me empty and unhappy, but I couldn't let go of my desire to act. Amma knew my heart and fulfilled my deepest desire in the best possible way.

My very last performance was a short play at Amma's retreat in San Ramon. I had one line... and the most Divine audience. I was finally a star: completely seen, loved and adored on every possible level. I felt Her love in the deepest depths of my soul.

All my life, I wanted nothing but theatre; but in that instant, the desire vanished entirely. I was free.

Amma took me out of the abyss of worldliness. I left the theatre, the parties, the money, and all those tarnished dreams behind. After that performance, I just didn't need them anymore; the desire was gone.

For me, beauty no longer comes wrapped in a movie star's shining silhouette. These days, I see beauty in Amma's hands – hands dedicated to serving the poor and needy, as they pull person after person into Her warm embrace.

I don't need to be a star anymore, all alone, glittering up in the sky. I've come down to earth, and these days, all I want to do is serve.

Amma has come to take us to our true home. This home is closer than the closest, but we have long forgotten where we are supposed to live, especially when we get lost in worldly pursuits and illusive dreams. Amma has returned to help us awaken to the inherent Divinity that lies dormant within us. Not by trying to make us

super human, but by making us **genuinely** human, helping us to realize our utmost potential.

Amma always regarded Her mother as Her guru. Amma's mother was incredibly strict, she always pointed out every mistake that Amma made – but Amma was grateful for this training. Because of Her mother's discipline, Amma was able to gain so much awareness right from an early age.

In the same way, Amma tries Her best to guide and protect us, but if we don't follow Her teachings, life will teach us our lessons the hard way – that's just how life is. All too often our desires get in the way and lead us down the wrong path.

Amma reminds us that in reality, the divine spark of pure love is so close to us. It is within every one of us, totally within our grasp. She is trying to inspire us to reach a little further beyond our desires so that we can understand the deeper meaning of life. This does not mean that we should stop striving to achieve our goals. We can still work for external accomplishments, but we should try to remember that they are only one very small part of life.

Amma wants us to understand that the real reward in life is so much more gratifying than simply achieving external name and fame.

Ultimately, 'We are love.' When we remember this truth, it will unlock hidden treasure inside our heart, and we will find what we were always looking for.

Chapter 3

Love Letter

To see things in the seed, that is genius.

– Lao Tzu

Many years ago, when my husband and I first moved to the Amritapuri ashram, things were much smaller. There were only a handful of departments: no recycling, no compost, no waste management and certainly no farms. There was simply no infrastructure to support such things.

One day at lunch, my husband and I got into an animated discussion with a friend about how to make the ashram more eco-friendly and sustainable.

Inspired by the conversation, we decided to write a letter to Amma expressing our desires. We listed a host of ideas: recycling, composting, organic gardening, selling organic herbs, and using solar panels… the list went on and on. We were so excited to share these ideas with Amma and were hopeful that She would give Her blessing to some of them.

We asked an Indian resident to help us translate the letter into Malayalam. As she read it, her mood quickly soured. It was clear that she was very upset by what she was reading. We were totally confused. Once she finished reading, she responded angrily that she would, "Absolutely NOT" translate the letter for Amma, as it was not our place to tell the Guru what to do. She gave us a good scolding and stormed away.

We had not intended the letter as a criticism in any way, and we definitely didn't mean to be telling Amma what to do. We simply wanted to ask Her if She thought any of these ideas would benefit the ashram, and if so, which ones to focus on.

We were so shocked and saddened by this person's response that we decided not to give Amma the letter at all. We didn't want to be disrespectful, and despite our best intentions, our letter seemed to be insulting. Feeling disheartened, I put the letter beneath my photo of the Goddess Lakshmi, on my altar.

Several months later, I was meditating near Amma on the European tour. When I opened my eyes, Amma looked at me, smiled, and beckoned me to Her side. She spoke to me in Malayalam, and the woman next to Her translated, "Amma says She really liked the letter you gave Her."

I was completely confused. I had not given Amma a letter on that tour. In fact, I hadn't given Her a letter that whole year. "Amma," I replied earnestly, "I didn't give you a letter." But Amma insisted that I *had* given Her a letter. Finally, I remembered the letter that my friend, my husband and I had written about our ideas for the ashram. The letter was still exactly where I had left it: beneath Lakshmi's picture on my altar.

I asked Amma if She was referring to the letter on my altar. She gave an enthusiastic, "Yes!" Amma then listed each one of the points we had written about, in very specific detail. Amma said She really liked all of these ideas, and was so happy we were thinking about how to live in greater harmony with Mother Nature.

I left that conversation filled with awe and bliss. How could Amma know the details of a letter She had never seen?

Over the years, each and every suggestion we made in that letter has come to fruition. The ashram has gone from burning garbage, to having a huge waste management department: we recycle virtually everything. There is a compost department supplying compost to fertilize the many farms around the ashram. We even have a Wellness Clinic where we sell organic herbs, many of which are grown in the ashram itself. Solar panels cover the roof of the bhajan hall, and organic vegetables are grown in every nook and cranny of the ashram.

Perhaps the most exciting thing is that our programs and activities are now being introduced outside of the ashram, to help uplift the world. Amma's Amrita Serve program is teaching organic farming methods in villages throughout India. The waste management department gives classes on recycling, organizes ABC (Amala Bharatam) cleanup days to pick up litter throughout India, and cleans sacred sites and rivers throughout India (including the holy Ganga River!).

Outside of India, many of Amma's ashrams in Europe, the USA and Canada, maintain organic vegetable gardens and fruit orchards, build permaculture farms, employ water-saving techniques, keep bees, and hold classes about sustainable agriculture.

Not only did Amma know our hearts, Her Grace has led to more environmental projects and initiatives than we could ever have imagined!

Since that amazing experience, I often write letters to Amma and leave them under Her photo on my altar. Even as I write the letter, I know that She already knows its contents.

When I unburden my heart to Amma, without fail, a perfectly clear answer always comes. Sometimes it comes in the form of a solution to a problem. Sometimes it comes in the form of a friend saying exactly what I need to hear.

No matter what the situation, whenever we reach out to Amma, She always answers back with overflowing love and grace.

Just as a child growing in the womb is nourished by the energy and nutrients flowing through the umbilical cord, so too is the grace and connection that we can share with Amma. Developing sincerity towards Amma, even only one second of it, gives Her an opening to reignite the inherent Divine power that lies within us.

Distance is no barrier when it comes to love. If we simply open our heart, we can enjoy a strong connection and feel the transmission of Her wisdom, guidance and grace, wherever we are in the world. This is the miraculous power of innocent selfless love.

Chapter 4

Learning to Smile

The heart is a thousand-stringed instrument
That can only be tuned with Love.

– Hafiz

My parents and I were immigrants, and we lived in a country that did not value differences. My family looked different, spoke a different language, ate different foods and had different customs and rituals. Suffice to say, growing up I never felt welcome.

When I was a baby, our home was on a small island. There were no roads, only ferries. There was only one school on the island, and every year at harvest time, the school emptied out so that the children could help their parents pick the crops. The locals had lived that way for centuries.

When I was old enough to start my education, my parents wanted me to attend school year-round, so they sent me to a different island. My whole childhood was spent like that: living in one place and going to school in another. To make matters worse, we moved each year from house to house and town to town.

I was lonely and terribly unhappy. Every time I made a friend, it was time to leave again. It became easier to stop making friends. The only thing the neighbours, teachers and other kids ever noticed about me was that I never smiled.

This deep-seated unhappiness remained as I matured. I suffered from severe depression, but it was never formally diagnosed. No one could figure out what was wrong with me.

As I grew into adulthood, I decided I wanted to do something about my overwhelming unhappiness. I knew I had a problem and I wanted to heal.

I tried all sorts of different things: I changed my job and my house over and over again. I tried Qi Gung, experimented with different diets, and visited a host of medical doctors – all of whom told me I was perfectly healthy. I participated in healing workshops and tried working with therapists and social workers. I looked into my family history to try and understand my parents better; and I volunteered in politics to try to make the world better.

Nothing worked.

Finally, I tried religion. I knocked on the door of every single monastery in my village – all 11 of them. I rang bell after bell, asking for a place to stay. 11 doors were slammed in my face. Over and over again, I was told, "There is no place for you here; get a room in the village."

In one monastery, the monk in charge allowed me to stay for one night. When he told me I was welcome, I burst into tears.

Out of options, I booked a plane ticket to India. I knew nothing about spirituality. All I knew was that I'd been rejected 11 times. But when I came to Amma, everything changed. Amma welcomed me with open arms. Although I had nothing to offer Her, She offered me a home.

Now She has started to work on me. She is teaching me and giving me understanding. Before I came to Amma I had been a mess. I was so weak. I wanted to be better, but I simply couldn't change.

Amma has taught me that holding onto pain is like clinging to a thorn bush while crying out desperately that it hurts. It is we who are unwilling to let go of our pain. That's how I was – that was my life.

I know for certain that Amma genuinely wants me to give up all of my suffering, even though I still cling to it so deeply sometimes. She wants me to be good and happy and to change – even more than I want it for myself. She showers me with more love than I have ever known, and loves me so much more than I am able to love myself.

Slowly and patiently, Amma is helping me transform. For the first time in my memory, because of Amma, I can smile.

⚜ ⚜ ⚜

We spend so much of our time agitated and in pain – worrying about the future or regretting the past. We search outside ourselves for happiness, thinking, 'If I could just find that elusive jewel, then everything would be okay.' But, somehow or another, that jewel always seems to stay just beyond our grasp…

It is very difficult to change our mindset, for doing so requires us to dwell fully in the present moment. Almost no one lives in the present (as simple as it seems, it is extremely challenging to do so) but shouldn't we at least try?

When we are able to dwell in the present, we will discover the glory of creation everywhere, even in the most insignificant places. It can be found right here – right in front of us – which is exactly where we least expect to find it.

Look at the wonder of an egg, or of a seed. The perfection of an apple...When we view life through the unjudging eyes of the present moment, then the happiness we are constantly seeking will bubble up from within.

At the airport recently, a few of us accompanied Amma in the lounge while we waited for our flight. After I had made sure that Amma was settled comfortably, I went back to pick up my bag, which I had left with a devotee. Along the way, I saw another devotee expectantly waiting for Amma in the boarding area. I told her not to bother waiting, as Amma would not be coming through that area again. We would be boarding directly from the airline lounge onto the plane. After exchanging a few words with her, I collected my bag and returned to the lounge to sit with Amma.

Suddenly, Amma stood up and announced that She wanted to go back to be with everyone else in the boarding area. I protested slightly, telling Her we were able to board the plane directly from the lounge. A mere

30 feet away was an exit door that led directly onto the aircraft. I did not want Amma to have to walk up and down the stairs unnecessarily. But Amma was insistent: "No. I want to be with my children for a while."

I was a bit slow to gather all of our bags, so Amma returned to the group alone. The devotee I had spoken with earlier was standing in the hallway by herself. To her amazement, Amma walked around the corner and greeted her.

When I walked past, two minutes later, the devotee just stared at me in ecstasy, blubbering syllables that I could not really understand. I wanted to listen, but I had to rush on to catch up with Amma.

A few days later, the devotee sent me an email explaining why she couldn't form a coherent sentence when I had seen her in the airport. Here is what she wrote:

"WOW, WOW, WOW! – What a Grace. I was alone with Amma for a few seconds. She greeted me, looked at me and touched my hand. I was in paradise; it felt like a blissful dream! What luck to be alone with Amma and then to travel on the same plane! I am still in ecstasy!"

When we find spirituality, it becomes the greatest treasure in our life. When we look at the world through the eyes of love, something small, like a simple touch and a few words can make our hearts soar. Being in Amma's physical presence brings us so much unimaginable joy and bliss. But Amma wants us to strive for that ultimate, lasting happiness within: the ability to be with Her all the time – in our heart.

When we put forth an effort to try and envision the Divinity in everyone and everything, no matter where life's circumstances may take us, we will find peace and bliss.

Chapter 5

Deciding to Serve

Thousands of candles can be lit from a single candle.

— The Buddha

My life had always been chaotic. I knew that I wanted to help people, but I could never figure out exactly how. It was a vague desire, somewhat confused and buried, but always present.

I started my professional career as a theatre teacher, which lasted for a few years. Then I moved onto a fishing boat and spent ten years living on the Mediterranean, spending my days and nights diving deep into the sea. Following that, I pursued a career as a sculptor. After three years, I decided to sell my studio; it was time to move on. At that point, I had the choice: I could either buy a car or spend a year and a half living with Amma in India. I chose India.

My time with Amma was extraordinarily beautiful. She opened my eyes. I finally had the opportunity to really serve, which was all I've ever really wanted. I knew that I would have to go back home eventually, and so, with only one month left until my departure, I posed a question to Amma. Inside my heart I had a deep desire to work with young people, but I still didn't know what I could do for them. I just knew that I wanted to help somehow.

I went onstage with my question ready:

"Dear Mother, I wish to serve you eternally, but I don't know exactly how right now. I love you."

The translator looked at me with raised eyebrows, "Are you sure you know what you are asking? You want to serve Amma *eternally*?"

I nodded.

"How do you want to serve?" she asked.

Then, in front of Amma, a project took shape in my mind. It was born in that moment. The idea arrived fully formed.

I was to create a house for young women who had nowhere else to go, for prostitutes, for girls who had been sexually abused. It would be a house for the outcasts of society, for children who had been thrown away by the system and whom nobody wanted. It would be a rehab centre and care home.

We would have a room for meditation; we would grow our own organic food and cook it ourselves. We would have workshops, sports and yoga classes. The girls would get private tutoring and regular therapy. It would be a safe place, a place where their pimps couldn't find them, a place where they would be free from drugs and abuse. It would be a happy place, full of transformation and healing.

When the idea was translated for Amma, She burst out with tremendous joy and laughter. The joy Amma expressed in that moment has been nourishing me ever since.

Whenever it has been difficult, whenever I have encountered obstacles, I have remembered Her laughter. Amma then told me that She had heard each one of my prayers, that the idea for the project had come from Her, and this was the exact project She wanted to create in France.

When I asked Her what to call it, Amma paused, as if looking into the future, and said that the name would come spontaneously when I found the house.

It was clear to me that Amma could see the place in Her mind's eye, that She could see the fulfilment of my dream. This feeling would be a great support for me in the difficult months to come.

When I returned to France, I immediately started working on the project. I created a website and started the process of securing funding. Then came the paperwork and the mountains and mountains of red tape.

I didn't have any money left, but instead of taking a job and focusing on my own needs (like I might have done in the past), I decided to continue working on my project full-time. Rather than rent an apartment, I lived with different friends, sleeping on one couch for a few nights and then moving on to another. When the need for money became desperate, I took short-term factory work to keep myself afloat. I felt Amma's presence the whole time; She was present in every single moment.

Every time I had an important phone call to make, I felt Amma standing there right next to me. Her Grace followed me every step of the way.

The next time I went for Amma's darshan, I gave Her a little tree as an offering. I desperately wanted Her to give me a tree in return – a tree to plant at the house. Instead, She gave me an apple. It was the first time She had ever given me an apple.

As I sat down to meditate after my darshan, I realized that She had given me the very tree I had been wishing for. There was exactly one seed in that special apple. When I returned to France, I planted it and waited, watching over it patiently.

The work continued. I searched for a house, carefully filled out all the government paperwork and put together a Board of Directors. Everything was in order, and on the morning of our very first board meeting, the little seed sprouted.

All I've ever truly wanted, all my life, was to pour my skills, my energy and my life into service. Before traveling with Amma, I didn't know what I could do, but Amma gave me vision. She inspired my imagination and strengthened my heart. I could never have done this without Her. Now I get to live my dream.

These girls don't know it yet, but they are Amma's children. Amma has blessed our future home, and I have faith in Her. Without Amma's grace, without Her strength – none of this would be possible.

I know there will be very difficult moments. We face many threats: suicide, violence and substance abuse (amongst others). But there will also be magical moments. When I see the place, I see joy. I see music, and I see dance. I see Amma's laughter on the faces of these girls, and I know that in time, the lives of these girls will be transformed.

Youth today are growing up in difficult times. The traditional value system has deteriorated so much in recent years, and because of this our children suffer. But Amma reminds us, so sweetly, that there is another way.

Amma is inspiring people, seed by seed, thought by thought, embrace after embrace to create a beautiful difference in the world. We all have the capacity to reach down to Mother Earth and share in Her joy by planting something beautiful – whether it is an apple seed or a community care-home.

If we let Amma plant the seed of selfless love in our heart, we will definitely experience a rich harvest of all the greatest blessings and joys that life can offer.

Chapter 6

Never Alone

*Doubt is a pain too lonely to know
that faith is his twin brother.*

– Khalil Gibran

When I was young I was a Christian, a Catholic to be precise. I was extremely devout but upset with the Church. I lived in a very wealthy community where the priests wore gold rings and watches and gave fancy sermons, but there was never talk of them giving money to the poor or helping at homeless shelters.

When I was 17, the Church held a community-wide meeting to talk about their funds and where the Church's money was going. I was the only person to attend. The pastor proudly showed me drawings of a big renovation project they had in mind for the Church. Almost all the money was going into expansion.

They intended to double the Church in size, expand the parking lot, add a gift shop and commercialize everything. I knew there were other churches in the neighbourhood doing the same thing. To me it seemed unnecessary and extravagant.

"What about charity?" I asked. "Don't we have any charities we help?" Although I went to church regularly, I had never once heard the pastor talk about giving to the poor.

"There is one hospital we give a little money to," he replied sheepishly. "Every month we give them a small contribution, but we aren't the only ones who support them. There is a large group of churches who work together to sponsor the hospital."

I left the Catholic Church.

The only other option was to attend one of the Protestant churches nearby. Where I grew up there were very few options: you were either a Christian or an atheist.

The Protestant churches were a lot more fun, alive with guitars and music. My friends started taking me to Christian rock concerts, which were amazing. The music was passionate, and at times quite spiritual. For the first time in my life I felt a real connection with a living, dynamic God. But I still wasn't satisfied.

I started talking to agnostics; they had a lot of really good arguments. When they asked me tough questions about God, I didn't have answers. I was still a Christian, but I was definitely confused about a lot of aspects of my faith. I wanted to feel closer to God. I knew I was seeking something, but I felt very far away from finding it.

My greatest desire was to be of service to the world somehow. It was very frustrating at the time because nobody understood why I wanted that. I didn't even know why I wanted that. Now, after meeting Amma it all makes much more sense.

When I went off to college, for the first time I was finally free to think for myself. At the same time, I was very lonely and started looking for a relationship. I wanted to find someone who could share my beliefs about spirituality.

Most of the people I met were either agnostic or extreme Christians; there was almost no middle ground. Then I met someone: a former Christian who (in my judgmental eyes) had given up his faith. He wasn't worried about going to hell or the after-life or anything like that. Instead, he spent his time meditating at home. I felt a tremendous desire to save him. After all, that's what Christians do – we save people.

My work was cut out for me. Here was someone who had studied the Bible. He had read it front to back. In fact, a few years earlier he had been one of those guys going around trying to convert people. Now he was just sitting in meditation at home, and so obviously not Christian anymore. I was completely perplexed by him; I couldn't figure it out. I thought something was wrong with him. But the truth is: I was the one who needed the help, not him.

We had a great time together for a few months. He never tried to save me. He didn't care about that. He just cared about me. We talked a lot about spirituality and he introduced me to new ideas and concepts. He gave me books about Jesus that made me see God in a whole new light. Most importantly, he taught me how to meditate. It was a very simple, non-dualistic type of meditation, and I really liked it.

I thought I could just be a meditating Christian. But my close friends from high school all started freaking out – totally freaking out. They sent me Bibles, lots of Bibles. One of them even made a video of her preschool class sitting together in prayer. She told me they were all praying for me and hoping I would come back to God – all because I had started meditating! It was so bizarre.

These were my closest friends, people I had known for years, but if I questioned their beliefs about Jesus, or even simply opened a discussion on the topic, they would get angry and upset and shut the conversation down. I was completely shocked.

They told me I was going to hell. It was all very black and white for them. My cousin told me, matter-of-factly, that if a baby died before she was able to accept Jesus into her heart, then that baby was going to hell. A baby? Where was the loving God in all of this?

I knew that my friends and family weren't thinking for themselves. They could easily recite the Bible scriptures, but when pressed, they couldn't tell you what the words meant. As soon as I began questioning them, they all turned against me.

It was around this time that I started to become friends with a woman I had met in my college classes. She was an Amma devotee, but unlike my high school friends, she was supportive and never tried to convert me. We became really close. Whenever she talked about Amma, which wasn't too often, I would usually make some connection with Jesus. She would just smile, and it was fine.

Eventually, she brought me to her satsang group. It was just a few people who gathered to sing bhajans and eat dinner together. My first impression: the people were nice enough, but the satsang was weird (really weird). These people were all worshiping a woman! There was only one thing I knew for certain: we should never worship anyone except for Jesus. I knew I would never go back. It was idolatry. It was wrong.

Honestly, I had only gone to the meeting to make my friend happy, but it wasn't for me.

Then I had one terrible night. My boyfriend and I had broken up a few weeks earlier, and I felt completely alone. The depression that had been hanging over my head since our breakup started taking over. I lay on my bed, sobbing.

Suddenly I felt afraid that I might hurt myself. I knew that I needed to get out of the room and go somewhere. I didn't know where to go, and I didn't particularly care where I ended up.

I started driving, blindly turning around corners, driving farther and farther away from the city. I was crying so hard that it was difficult to see. I had no idea where I was, or where I was going. After some time I found myself in the countryside, when all of a sudden I recognized the place.

I was at the Amma Centre where my friend had taken me months before. Honestly, I didn't know how to get there, but that's where the car had somehow ended up.

It was one or two in the morning when I arrived. The place was completely deserted.

I went to the only building I saw and tried the door. It was unlocked; I was so surprised. The big, empty room was almost entirely bare except for a giant picture of Amma. The solitary light shined on Her face.

I didn't know anything about Amma, who She was or what it all meant. But She had the sweetest smile. As I sat in front of that photo sobbing, I poured my heart out to Her and told Her all of my problems.

It really felt like She was listening. Somehow, I knew She could hear me. There was a tangible presence in the room, and I felt comforted. All I wanted was for Her to hold me.

In the corner of the room there was a tiny little store with a table full of the cutest little Amma dolls.

I never had a big attraction to dolls before, not since I was six years old, but I had an overwhelming desire for an Amma doll of my own.

I picked one up and held her in my arms for a long time. It felt as though Amma Herself was hugging me through the doll. I had to have her. I checked how much money I would owe the Centre and took her home.

By the time I got back to my apartment, the sun was rising. I collapsed onto my bed and fell asleep clutching my little Amma to my heart. When I woke up later that morning, I felt so much better. The depression was almost completely gone. From then on whenever I felt sad, I would hold that little doll, and I knew that everything would be okay.

I can't say that my pain all disappeared that night, or that from then on, all my problems evaporated instantly, but there certainly was a major shift. From that night onwards, I have always felt a deep, deep courage and strength inside myself, stemming from the knowledge that Amma is always with me.

Amma is always listening to our hopes and dreams, our pain and our prayers. She understands us more deeply than we understand ourselves.

She can see through the darkest night, right into our very souls – even if all we can feel are the inner walls of separation and pain keeping us apart. Even when we can't feel Her presence, we should remember: no matter what, She is always with us.

Years ago, when we were traveling on a train in India, Amma mentioned that everything She does has a meaning. She said this in the middle of the night, somewhere on a train ride between New Delhi and Calcutta.

As the train pulled into a station, chanting rose up from the platform: "Om Amriteshwaryai Namaha… Om Amriteshwaryai Namaha…"

Devotees had gathered there yearning for a glimpse of Amma. She stood up and ran to the door of the carriage, eager to see them.

"Can you open it?" She asked. The latch was stuck – but suddenly, the latch became unstuck, and Amma was able to smile at the gathered crowd…but it only lasted a moment. As soon as the train began to move, the door slammed shut again.

Amma was not finished. She pressed Her face up against the window and smiled lovingly at everyone on the platform. Love poured through that train window; only a thin piece of glass kept Amma apart from the devotees. The crowd surged forward, reaching out to touch Her, or at least to touch the glass between them. She pressed Her hand against the window, matching it to one man's palm, which was pressed up against the other side of the glass. Then again, a woman's hand was 'touched' through the glass.

As the train slowly pulled out of the station, we returned to Amma's compartment. There, the window glass was dark. The devotees could not see Amma, but Amma could see them. She saw everyone following after the train, calling out to Her. Some raised their hands over their heads in farewell while others strained to touch the glass because, at least, it was Her window…

"This is how the world is," Amma said as She watched them. "I can see them, but they can't see me. The Guru sees everything and everyone, but no one really sees the Guru."

Chapter 7

You Did Good

*Life's most persistent and urgent question
is: 'What are you doing for others?'*

– Martin Luther King

I meant to wake up early and get to Amma's program first thing, but of course that didn't happen; I slept in. A friend called and woke me up late that morning. "Where are you?" she asked. "Are you coming?" Amma was visiting LA, and I was going to meet Her for the first time.

I jumped out of bed, rushed to the program site, and arrived about 11 a.m. My token number was ZZYZ, or something crazy like that, and the local volunteers told me I probably wouldn't get my darshan until something like 3 a.m. the following morning. I had a lot of time to fill, so I started exploring.

The first thing I noticed was all of the volunteer activities and charities Amma runs. I love volunteering, so I spent a fair bit of time reading all about Amma's service projects. Then I noticed the shop: a shopping centre here? I was so excited. At that moment the band began to play…a shopping centre and a band? I was in heaven.

I didn't know what this place was, but I already loved it.

My friend waved me over. She had saved me a seat about ten rows from where Amma was sitting. The guy beside me was also new and we chatted for a little while. I turned to look at Amma. All of a sudden the people in front of Her moved away. It was as if the Red Sea was parting.

She looked directly at me and smiled.

The feeling of pure love from Her gaze swept over my entire body. I felt as if I was being wrapped in the softest cotton. I remember thinking, 'This feels like love, but it's not like any love I've ever felt before.' I absolutely needed to get closer. I squirmed my way to the front row behind the band. I sat and stared at Amma; the longer I stared, the more my heart filled up. I sat rooted to that spot for seven hours straight, unblinking.

I went back to the program every day while Amma was in LA. The morning after She left, I woke up and my mind was spinning: 'What do I do now?' I asked myself. It wasn't enough just to see Amma again someday; I wanted to see Amma again *every* day. All I wanted was to be with Her. I spent hour after hour contemplating how to make this happen.

I felt sad and overwhelmed after She left and needed to bring myself back down to earth again. 'Well, maybe I'll go shopping,' I thought to myself. 'That always works.' So I bought a coffee and went to the mall to buy some shoes. I sat on the couch in the shoe store thinking, 'What is this?' The whole experience seemed a lot less enticing than it had before.

I wandered the aisles a bit and eventually found a few pairs of shoes that I liked, but every couple of minutes I would stop dead in my tracks and start daydreaming about Amma again. 'What am I doing?' I asked myself. 'Why am I wasting my time buying these shoes? I just want to be with Her.'

As I walked towards the checkout counter, a girl stopped me. She pointed to the shoes I was holding and said, "I love those shoes. Where did you get them?" I pointed back towards the rack where I had found them. We started talking.

She confided that she had a wedding to go to in two hours and didn't own any nice shoes. "I hate shopping," she told me. "I feel so lost and over-whelmed in these huge department stores." She thanked me for pointing her in the right direction, and we went our separate ways.

As I finished paying the cashier, the girl walked over again. She asked the woman behind the counter if there was another pair of shoes like the ones I had just bought.

"That's the last pair," the saleswoman responded flatly. Her shoulders sagged slightly as she walked away, looking a little sad and confused.

Then suddenly, out of nowhere, a strange thought yelled itself into my mind, 'Don't let that girl leave the store! Go give her your shoes!'

'What? No way! I'm not doing that!'

The thought came back even more loudly. 'Don't let that girl leave the store! Go get her and give her your shoes!'

'No!' I told myself firmly. 'I am absolutely *not* going to go running after that girl. That is too weird. I am keeping my shoes.'

The thought came again. It would not be ignored.

I looked around for a few minutes, half-heart-edly attempting to find her. She was nowhere to be seen. Convinced she had left the store, I let out a sigh of relief.

Then she walked back in.

What could I do? I walked over to her and said, "Here, take my shoes. You need them more than I do." She looked at me, completely horrified, as if I had grown two heads or something. "That is so weird. I can't do that. They're yours!"

"Yeah, but you are the one going to a wedding in two hours, not me. I was just buying them for the sake of buying them. You actually need them. I don't." She didn't say anything. "Look, it's not weird. We are not going to make it weird. Just take the shoes, and try them on."

She looked at me for a moment, "Really…?" The shoes fit perfectly. She was clearly elated, but looked at me shyly, "Are you sure?"

"Listen, this is not open for discussion." I rolled my eyes, "You have to take them."

All of a sudden, I was overcome by a huge tingling sensation that vibrated throughout my entire body. It was the exact same feeling I'd had during my first darshan with Amma. It all became clear: 'This is it! This is Amma's teaching.'

She smiled happily and said, "This is one of the nicest things that anyone has ever done for me…and I don't even know you. I'm going to tell this story to everyone at the wedding. From now on, every time I look in my closet, I am going to remember your kindness, and it's going to remind me to be kind too."

It was the simplest thing, one small gesture in a department store in LA, a single pair of shoes…but it was more than that. In that moment, Amma was there. I felt like I had received Her darshan.

What I understood in that moment, is that this one small act of giving truly creates a ripple effect.

Despite my big revelation, I was still totally ungrounded, so I did the only thing that made sense: I went shopping again. This time I went to the Apple store.

Again, just like at the shoe store, there I was sitting with my coffee in hand thinking, 'Wait, what just happened?'

I turned. Standing next to me was a little girl who looked exactly like Amma. She had the same skin colour, the same hair, the same eyes and the exact same nose. She climbed up on the stool beside me and sat with her hand on her chin in the exact same way Amma often does. She looked into my eyes and smiled.

I knew precisely what Amma was telling me..."You did good."

❦ ❦ ❦

It is important to think about others, and not only what we need or want in our own lives. Spirituality is so practical: down to earth and practical. It is just the good, simple common sense that we all hold inside of us.

Amma teaches us to use the discrimination that is already within us. We all have the intuition to know right from wrong. If we simply follow that, while trying to help – and not hurt other people – then we will intuitively know the correct way to behave.

Amma often points out that if we do not put compassion into our actions, then even the word 'love' will only ever remain a lifeless word. We will never be able to experience true love until our heart can melt in compassion for others.

Sometimes when we sacrifice our own needs to help someone else, we actually gain more than when we simply take for ourselves. When we do good deeds for others our heart opens up, making room for Amma to step inside.

Chapter 8

Finding Love

*Darkness cannot drive out darkness; only
light can do that. Hate cannot drive
out hate; only love can do that.*

– Martin Luther King Jr.

I have the most amazing mother. She has always
been there for me. She has doted on me, loved me
and cared for me with all her heart. My father? He
used to beat her. She cried sometimes, but she never complained. I think there was a part of her that
always believed she deserved it.

My father never hit me, but he never seemed
to like me very much either. I was never, ever good
enough for him, and there was nothing I could do
that could make him happy.

One day at school, when I was about eight years
old, I finally did something to be proud of. Our
teacher returned our book-reports...mine had an

A+ scrawled in large red letters across the top. I was so excited. Finally, I had something I could show my father.

He took the paper, frowning. As he read my two-page essay, written out carefully in my very best handwriting, his frown only deepened. "Here," he said. "Here! You made a mistake." I had spelled one word wrong. He was furious and grounded me for three days.

Then, when I was 12, my father just left. For the first time in years, I could breathe: no more violence, no more fear. I remember riding home on the school bus and for the first time in my life, my stomach didn't turn with anxiety.

I got a boyfriend. Then another. From the ages of 12 to 26 (when I met Amma) I always had at least one man in my life. Usually I had two boyfriends at the same time, just to be safe. That way, if either one left me I wouldn't be alone. Sometimes my men knew about each other, sometimes they didn't. I didn't care.

Mostly I just wanted company, but they always expected more. I offered it. I figured it was payment for services rendered – the service of keeping that terrible, looming sense of loneliness at bay. I felt like I owed them for their friendship.

I hated myself, detested myself – passionately. I figured everyone else would too; at least once they got to know me. I was angry and violent, just like my father. I spent all of my time attempting to fulfill my base desires. My world was full of enemies; my only friends had to be bribed with favours.

My life was going nowhere and nothing held my interest. I quit my education and hated every job I ever tried. Despite the fact that I was in two (or sometimes three) committed relationships, I felt completely alone.

One night I hit rock bottom. As I lay on the floor of my flat, sobbing, I cried out to God, "You have to save me! You have to get me out of here! I can't do this anymore…"

That's when Amma arrived.

A friend of mine was a devotee. When Amma came to Europe he called me everyday, harassing me to go and meet Her. He was persistently annoying. Just to shut him up, I agreed to ask my boss for the time off. I knew she would say no. The restaurant where I worked was busy and completely under-staffed. We were already working 18-hour days.

When I asked, my boss looked at me, obviously surprised by my request. "Will it do you good?" she asked.

What could I say? I told her, "Well, my friend calls me everyday to tell me it will…"

"Are two days enough, or do you need more?"

My jaw dropped.

I arrived at the program a few days later, feeling on edge and skeptical. I took a seat in front and waited for this 'Amma' person to arrive.

When She walked into the hall, all I could see was light. It was a huge, bright energy, even bigger than the hall itself. The light seemed to move around Her tiny little body. It radiated from Her, but was not confined to Her.

After my darshan with Amma, I was able to relax for the first time in years. I cried the whole night.

I knew I had found God.

I used to think I was stubborn, but with Amma I met my match. She has forced me to transform, despite all my best efforts to self-destruct.

The first change She brought to my life was totally upsetting. Overnight, I became incredibly unattractive to men. Both of my boyfriends broke up with me, one right after the other. It was horrible.

That's when I made a female friend – then two. I was always so scared of women because I could never manipulate them. Now, for the first time in 15 years, I had people in my life I could talk to with no strings attached.

The weirdest part was, they genuinely seemed to like me.

A few months after I first met Amma, I visited Her ashram in India and saw girls working 18-hour days in the kitchen, just like I did, but, unlike me, they seemed totally thrilled about it. I pulled one of them aside, "Do you really work all day and *like it…?*"

I was shocked that anybody would *choose* to work. Back then; if I had my choice, I never would have lifted a finger.

When I started doing seva, for the first time in my life I found something that actually held my interest. I love seva; it feels like opening the floodgates of grace. Whenever I have a problem, I just do seva, and it always makes me feel a little bit better.

Amma supports me and carries me, no matter how hard I fight, or how many terrible things I've done. She is committed to me, despite my many mistakes and indiscretions. She knows me on the deepest level of my soul – and She doesn't hate me. She loves me just the way I am.

I no longer desperately seek out men to love me. Amma has filled the gaping hole in my empty heart. I know that I am loved unconditionally, and this awareness has helped me to begin to love myself.

The mind is full of fleeting thoughts and emotions, but this does not mean that we have to act on them. Everyone has desires; desire in itself is not the problem. The problem arises when we act on those desires in ways that hurt others and ourselves.

When we are in pain, wounded or angry, we are particularly susceptible to our own reactivity and poor decision-making. It is especially difficult at these times to act clearly, with discrimination. Nonetheless, it is important that we try to respond carefully to situations, in order to avoid doing something that we may regret later.

Remember why you came to this Earth, and do not let yourself make harmful choices! When we engage in harmful behaviours, the person we hurt the most is our self.

When bad things happen, people sometimes assume that God is cruel. They lose their faith, complaining, "What kind of God would allow for so much suffering?" But Amma understood, even as a young girl, that with every action we perform, a reaction is created. Sometimes these reactions take lifetimes to manifest, but our actions will always come back to us.

There is no escaping our karma, but it is important to remember that the unfathomable cycle of karma is always trying to teach us something good. When our karma comes back to us in the form of a rude or painful experience, it should serve to awaken us from the deep sleep of ignorance. God is not cruel; the Divine is only ever trying to bless us or shake us from the wrong path.

It is sometimes said that the Guru is greater than God because God will give us only what we deserve (to help us grow). The Guru, on the other hand, will offer only love and forgiveness. We can see this so clearly in Amma: the way She interacts with the thousands who come to Her every day. She is a flow of God's love in this world. She accepts us, with all of our human frailties. She uplifts us and takes us on the path towards the goal of human existence.

Amma is an incarnation of love. She came here out of pure compassion for our suffering. No matter how many mistakes we make, Amma loves us. She patiently and persistently encourages us to be like the lotus flower – to grow out of the mud and reach the sunlight.

Chapter 9

Becoming Arjuna

Ring the bell that still can ring,
Forget your perfect offering.
There is a crack in everything,
That's how the light gets in.

– Leonard Cohen

I was a lonely child. I had no friends, and my parents both worked all the time. They always hired someone to take care of me, so I was clean and well fed and so-forth, but I always felt alone.

My mother worked day and night. When she was home she spent all of her time in her office. I was only allowed to sit with her if I kept as quiet as a mouse: no whispering, no shuffling, no pencil scratching, and no sneezing. It would have been difficult for anyone – much less a hyperactive child. If I swallowed too loud, I might get kicked out.

One day, when I was five years old, an eyelash fell onto my cheek. My mother picked it up and with a smile said, "Make a wish."

Wishes could come true from eyelashes?

I started making wishes. I wished and I wished and I wished.

By the time I was 12, all my wishes were used up. My eyelashes had become bare. I moved onto my eyebrows. My parents didn't notice, but the school nurse did. She called home, and I was put into therapy.

It didn't work.

I moved onto my head. I was 13 when I developed my first bald spot, right in the back of my scalp – like an old man. I wasn't making wishes anymore, but there was an odd feeling of comfort when I pulled out my hair. Like an old friend, it kept me company and soothed me. I didn't know any other way to calm the ever-present anxiety.

I didn't get a haircut from the age of 13 to 18. I was too embarrassed. Only once did my mother insist. She told the hairdresser over the phone that I had leukemia; this way we wouldn't have to be embarrassed by my bald spots. I threw a fit. Needless to say, we didn't make it to that appointment. She gave up after that.

In college I cut my hair off with the help of scissors and a mirror. It was the only thing that helped reduce the craving to pull. It started to feel as if a vile, evil energy was living on top of my head. It was thick, nasty and sticky. It felt as if a demon was sitting up there, and I couldn't stand it. Cutting my hair off was the only way to stave off the addiction to pull. It was the only relief I had.

I often dreamed of having long, beautiful, thick hair, like when I was a child, but I knew I would never get there – not with lifetimes of effort. I was incurable.

I tried everything, every type of therapy: behavioural therapy, talk therapy, addiction therapy. "Sorry," one doctor told me. "Maybe you should try a different doctor. It *never* takes this long." I tried shamans. I tried magic. I even tried exorcisms. Nothing worked. For 20 years, nothing worked.

Then I met Amma.

At first nothing changed, and my addiction remained as strong as ever. When the cravings got bad, I still shaved my head with scissors. My head was littered with thick bald spots, and I suspect I looked really funny with the centimetre-long buzz cuts I gave myself.

One summer, about a year after I'd first met Amma, my mala broke. I was traveling with Amma at the time and decided to make two matching bracelets from the beads: one for me, and one for Her. I admit that they were pretty horrendous, but I thought they were stunning. I had made them with so much devotion. Honestly, they were bracelets only a mother could love. I wore them both while I waited for my darshan.

Then I wore them into the bathroom…

All of a sudden I was engulfed in a river of shame. I was overwhelmed with revulsion, sickened. How could I give Amma a gift I had just worn in the bathroom?

I choked when I thought about the dreadfulness of my error. I couldn't tell anyone, it was horrifying and embarrassing. I just knew that if anyone found out, they would be disgusted with me. I was filthy and my gift was filthy. I was sick to my stomach at the thought of giving the Divine Mother something so impure.

I didn't know what to do. I had made that bracelet especially for Her, with so much love. Finally, after much agonizing, I decided that I had to give the bracelet to Amma anyway. What else could I do?

I brought all my shame up to Amma and put it on Her wrist.

I whispered to Amma with child-like excitement, "Amma, now we are matching!" She pulled me in close. I heard Her reply inside my heart, 'We need to match on the inside.' In that moment all of my shame disappeared. I literally felt it rise up and leave. Suddenly I knew, beyond a shadow of a doubt, that I didn't need to pull out my hair anymore.

I stopped.

20 years of effort and nothing had worked... nothing. But in one darshan, Amma took it all away. 20 years of shame and guilt, 20 years of secrets and lies – all vanished in that one, single hug.

I can't say that I am perfect all the time. I still do pull out a few hairs here and there. On rare occasions, the addiction comes back, and I find myself at war again. In those moments, the demons of depression and shame both rear their ugly heads, but it is nothing like it used to be.

Before that darshan, I kept my hair short, always above my chin, usually closely cropped to my head. For years I walked through life with no eyebrows or eyelashes. I struggled daily with the intense, over-whelming desire to pull out my own hair. Sometimes I would stay awake for hours and hours, until the early hours of the morning, battling with my addiction. I always lost. I couldn't stop.

Then suddenly, there was no more fight. It was over, finished. Done.

For just one moment, I was Arjuna, and Krishna was my charioteer.

We won.

Amma is trying to release us from the prison cell of our minds. She has already unlocked the door, but we are often too afraid to step out. Instead of coming into the light, we keep redecorating our lonely cells with imaginary fears and pain.

Amma's love has no boundaries. But our self-imposed walls keep us from receiving love. It is extremely difficult to break out of the self-created shackles that bind us. Amma once said that we all want to be free, but even after She gives us a taste of freedom we put ourselves right back into the familiar chains that keep us bound.

Fortunately, Amma never gives up on us.

Amma openly loves everyone with pure, unconditional love. She accepts each one of us with all of our shame, pride, anger, fear and other frailties. Over time, the filter of Her love purifies our weaknesses and turns them into strengths.

*Deep inside, most of us have longed for a sweet, lasting love our entire lives. Amma gives us the unwavering motherly love we have always longed for. She is the mother most of us secretly wish our birth mothers could have been. She **is** our mother, our **real** mother, and She helps us to understand that love is the very source of life.*

Chapter 10

Overcoming Violence

"Yesterday I was clever, so I wanted to change the world. Today I am wise, so I am changing myself."

— *Rumi*

My mother was 17 when she got pregnant. She gave birth just after her 18th birthday. No one knew who my father was, and the mystery surrounding my birth was a source of deep shame for my entire family. He could have been anyone: the postman, the policeman, or the trash collector...she never told anyone. I was born without a father, which created a deep identity crisis within me.

The first nine years of my life were simple and sweet. My grandmother looked after me while my mother went to work. I spent long hours alone, climbing trees and hiding in secret places around our farm.

Then my mother fell in love with a military man, we moved to the city and everything changed.

My grandmother fell into a depression, and so did I. My new school was full of violence. At the age of nine, I learned to fight. My only friends were two gypsies who lived nearby.

I remember when I first arrived: an older boy cornered me against a wall, intending to punch me in the face. Miraculously, I managed to grab his hand. My fingers were small, but I held onto one of his thick fingers and bent it back…and back…and back…we heard a sickening crack.

He never bothered me again.

The bullies maintained a particularly violent ritual at my school: whenever a new boy joined the class, the kids would pin his arms and legs behind his back and bash his body into a concrete pillar. They would laugh as he screamed.

I could never stand by and do nothing when someone was being bullied, so I used to rush to the defense. I got lots of beatings in return. The other children put worms in my clothes and set my hair on fire. I was touched in all the wrong places. I got slapped, I got punched, and I had a knife held under my chin. My glasses were broken. My nose was bloodied.

I had no God. My grandmother used to take me to church sometimes, but the priest was beating my cousin, so when he preached loving kindness, I never believed him. I used to write in the dust, 'Nobody loves me.' I didn't trust in my mother's love because she still refused to tell me who my father was. My heart constantly hurt; I was angry all the time. The needless violence, the suffering, it was all too much.

I did the only thing that made sense: I ran away.

When I was still a teen, I went to live and work in very rich people's houses to support myself. Some of my employers were beautiful and famous. They had gorgeous children, spent their holidays on fancy vacations and had everything they wanted, but even so, they were miserable, just like the rest of us – so what was the point? Life was losing its meaning.

The older I grew, the more tasteless and colourless life seemed to become. I was angry at the world for all of the violence: for the needless suffering we inflict upon each other. Nothing was beautiful. Nobody was inspiring. Everything was just fake.

I didn't believe in love.

I was convinced that people only pretended to love each other in order to get something. I tried to shorten my lifespan in a natural way: I drank two litres of coffee and smoked two packs of cigarettes a day. I was miserable.

At some point, things shifted. I started to understand that the problem was within me. How could I expect someone to be something that I could not be myself? Instead of focusing on the faults of others, I decided to try to change myself.

I started therapy. At the suggestion of my therapist I signed up for a 'healing workshop.' It focused on awakening the inner child and healing the 'father story.' It was exactly what I was looking for.

The man running the workshop focused a lot of attention on me. He invited me to come (for free!) to his next workshop about spirituality. I started traveling with him and helping him with his work. We grew very close and he became like a father to me.

A year or so after I started this work, I was with a friend one day and casually asked her, "What are you doing this weekend?"

"I'm going to see Amma," she replied.

I felt something I had never felt before – a stirring, deep within my heart.

"I'm going too." I replied matter-of-factly. I didn't even ask who Amma was or what She was doing. Something in me just knew I had to meet Her.

When I told my teacher where I was going, he tried to dissuade me; he complained, "But I'm a realized master too!"

I said nothing. I loved him so much, but I knew I had to go.

I arrived early to the program the next day and was one of the first people in the line. The energy in the darshan hall was uplifting; the air felt so pure. When I went up to Amma, She looked at me and laughed and laughed. I stared at Her, completely stunned. Suddenly I found the whole thing very funny too, and I laughed along with Her.

I stayed at the program the whole three days. Tears flowed from my eyes the entire time. I wasn't feeling sad, that wasn't it. I was just crying non-stop. I can't really explain it. When those three days were over, I felt totally renewed, different on every level: physical, emotional and spiritual.

The most striking change was that my anger and pain about not knowing my father complete-ly vanished. The horrible, dreadful pain that had ripped through my heart on a daily basis – was gone. I had tried everything to heal that wound, and nothing worked, until I met Amma. In those three days, the crisis I had dealt with for years simply evaporated.

I still have my insecurities, my fear of being rejected and things like that. But I never again had the painful yearning to know his name, to see his face or to meet him. I no longer felt abandoned, and I no longer felt furious with my mother, who had denied me the truth. My relationship with her has started to heal.

When I met Amma, I knew that the love I was dreaming of actually existed. My whole life took on meaning that day. I realized that SHE is what I had been seeking all along.

Amma often instructs us to love and to serve however we can. I do my best to follow Her teachings. She has inspired a radical shift in my perspective and given me purpose. She helps me find opportunities to give, and in doing so, dispels darkness from my life (and hopefully from the lives of those around me). I suspect it must be working, as these days my boss often tells me that I have too much compassion for our customers!

People are no longer threatening enemies. Amma has transformed the difficulties in my life from miserable burdens into tools I can use for spiritual development. I have become better able to see challenges as opportunities, rather than overwhelming hurdles. When Amma lit that one small candle inside of my heart, the darkness in the world seemed so much less frightening.

Today my birth mother is a good friend – that was entirely Amma's grace. As soon as I was able to get over my anger, our relationship transformed. Recently I wrote her a letter of gratitude: "Thank you. Thank you for bringing me into this world. Thank you for keeping me, even though you were so young and times were so hard. I love that every single day I can find opportunities to grow, to learn and most importantly, to serve. Thank you – because I love this world, and I love my life."

Amma dwells in a constant state of selfless love. She is inviting all of us to join Her there. When we

serve others, a little bit of Amma's energy and grace transfers to us.

Amma sets the perfect example. She shows us that no matter how dark the world around us may seem, we can experience a profoundly exquisite joy and happiness when we strive to live a life devoted to selflessly giving and serving.

It's not as though we have to do some big, important things. There is always someone ready to tackle a problem when it is viewed as "important." Rather, it is the little things we do (like picking up trash or cleaning someone's dish) that bring satisfaction and joy into our lives. If we can be happy doing small acts of service such as these, we will find a deep sense of contentment (and things really will get cleaned up nicely).

Amazing though it may seem, when we give something away with a resolve of pure love, there is no sacrifice. In fact, for spiritual seekers, hard work and loss can actually become a tremendous source of enjoyment (despite a few blisters and aching muscles along the way).

In my life, the sweetest, most wonderful blessings have flowed from Amma, who has given me the chance to serve Her charities. Not everyone can come to India to do service, but no matter where we are in the world, life presents us with so many chances to serve. When we do so, the floodgates of grace open up, and life becomes a magnificent adventure.

Chapter 11

Despair of a Broken Heart

*Our greatest glory is not in never falling,
but in rising every time we fall.*

– Confucius

I was born in an ashram and lived a spiritual life until I was 16. As a child I always felt happy and complete. Our ashram was a quiet place. We had very little, but we were content.

The community beside our ashram was like a different world. Many affluent people flitted around the streets. Our next-door neighbour was Ringo Starr's son. I grew up amidst a lot of rich and famous people, but never felt a part of their world.

Some of my friends were so drawn to the material world that they would buy new "toys" every month – a new car, a new boat, a new drug.

Most of my peers at school started partying, behaving promiscuously and getting involved with drugs by the age of 12, but I always managed to stay away from all of that. I knew the true nature of life. I didn't need those things; my heart was full.

Then, overnight, everything changed. When I was 16 my Guru died, and my whole life collapsed. I remember the day he died so clearly. I was completely inconsolable and couldn't stop crying. My mother and brothers all felt the same, so we were unable to comfort each other. We were all lost. In one instant, everything we had, everything we trusted and put faith in, completely vanished from our lives.

I now understand that pain as attachment to a form, but never before had I known a form so perfect as his. His every word, breath and action was in perfect harmony with creation. He was my dearest friend, my father and my Master – always there to guide me, to show me the road to my own salvation. I could never imagine that anyone in the world could ever replace him. I held him in the highest respect, love and trust.

The loss sent me into a downward spiral. I went crazy.

I was desperate to numb the pain – to fill the gaping hole in my heart. His loss left me empty inside. I didn't want to live anymore. If the entire world held only illusory material pursuits and empty fruitless goals, then I saw no reason to continue.

I started taking intoxicants and began to live life very much on the edge, just to give it some meaning. I said, "Yes," to anything that came along, no matter how dark or dangerous. I joined the world of my peers. In their reality God did not exist: we were the Gods. My friends and I thought we were above everything, including the law. We lived dangerously and did whatever we wanted.

We were the worst possible teenagers you could imagine.

My mom was very concerned about me and began searching for a new Master, someone in the physical body. She felt that it was very important to find someone who could teach us and guide us.

In 2001, her prayers were answered when she came across a poster of Amma. She went to the program and returned so excited. "Amma is the same," she told us. "She has the same teachings and the same energy. You have to come and see Her!"

But my heart was closed. I didn't want to open up to a new Guru; it was too painful. I refused to go to the program. The following year Amma returned. Somehow my mother managed to drag me along. I refused to go for darshan, but I sat and watched Amma for hours.

I felt dirty when I looked at Her, remembering all the things I had done to myself. I could sense Her spiritual greatness and knew I was unworthy to receive Her darshan.

People dressed in white kept coming up to me, asking the same annoying question, "Have you had darshan?" They kept pushing, but I really didn't want to go. I didn't want to get a hug from some Indian lady I didn't know. But after about three hours, I realized that the only way these people were going to stop bugging me was if I went for darshan.

When Amma took me into Her arms, I experienced a vast, empty, endlessly full black space. It didn't make any sense, but it triggered a memory in me. When I used to meditate with my first Guru I would often have blissful meditations of deep, vast emptiness.

Amma's darshan served as a bridge, connecting me back to how I used to feel in his presence: full of untainted purity and inconceivable innocence. Those trusted memories came flooding back in an instant.

It felt as though Amma had cleared away my karmic burden – She cleansed me. I did not understand who Amma was, but I did begin to remember my own wholeness.

While that first darshan was beautiful, it was not enough to transform my life. Things got even rockier as I sunk further into bad company. I associated with people whose only interest was pleasure seeking. These people were of a very dark nature, and we started engaging in criminal activities.

I started to reflect on where my life was going: I was slipping into darkness.

One night my friends threw a huge party on a yacht. They had exacted a nasty revenge on someone and decided to celebrate with a mountain of drugs.

I decided I was going to leave this planet. I was done with life.

I didn't want to associate with these people anymore or live an empty, meaningless existence. I wanted to end it all. I didn't see any other way out, so I decided to take an overdose.

I went down to the bottom of the boat. It was the middle of winter.

I lay down on the ice-cold metal and allowed the cold to seep deep inside my body. First my toes went numb, then my calves. Slowly the chill crept upwards. I lost sensation in my hands, and finally, I felt my heart go still. I could feel only one tiny bit of consciousness left, one small warm space inside my mind. Then that too vanished, and I was gone.

At once an amazing bright light surrounded me. It was indescribable, filling all dimensions. I felt immense joy and relief. All I wanted was to leave everything behind and merge with the Universal Consciousness, that brilliant light of lights.

As I started going deeper into the light, a figure appeared, very small at first, but it started getting bigger until it was human sized. On the edge of death, my first Guru had come to greet me.

When I was a child living in his ashram, he used to wake us up by ringing a little bell each morning and saying, "Wake up! Wake up! It's time to wake up!" This time he rang the bell and said, "It is *not* time now! Wake up! Wake up!"

All the light was pushed back into my body. I jumped up and stumbled off the boat. All I could think was, 'I have to get home. I have to get home!'

I called my mom and pleaded, "Please, please pick me up." It was 3 a.m., but my mom got in the car and drove two hours to come get me.

I knew then that I had to drastically change my life.

Amma came to my city two weeks later.

I wanted to ask if there was anything I could do to help Amma's organization or Her charities, but I was too shy to bother anybody with my stupid question. Within two minutes, I met someone who (despite my objections) dragged me up to Amma and told Her, "Amma, this boy wants to help."

Amma gave me a very sweet look; Her eyes were shining. She asked, "Can you come to India?"

I had never thought about it before, but I knew that this was my chance.

That was 11 years ago.

It's difficult to know how much spiritual progress I've made over the years, but I can say this: I recently met up with one of my very close friends from years before. He has been an addict for all the years that I have been in India. He has all the same friends, and his life is basically the same as it was 11 years ago. Seeing his deterioration was mind-blowing: he was not able to talk normally, his speech was slurred, he couldn't stop fidgeting, itching or scratching himself, and his mind was clearly very agitated. He could barely function.

I realized then…that would have been me (if I had even survived that long).

I can see now that a life spent in the Guru's presence can alter one's whole destiny. Such is the power of a fully realized soul. Amma has kept me so busy and focused on seva that I have not had time to entertain or chase other less-fruitful paths.

I finally feel peaceful again – and the desire to indulge in intoxicants is completely absent.

Amma is the greatest blessing in my life. If it had been anyone else, anything else, I know I would have fallen back on old habits.

Amma's love and guidance have held me and transformed me. She creates an atmosphere and an environment that is all-encompassing, fulfilling and embracing – so you don't need anything else. I give thanks to Amma every single day for who She is and what She does. All other accomplishments of the world seem to pale, in comparison to a life spent serving such a being.

Amma has said that the vibrations of a worldly environment alone are enough to pull us down, which is why we really need to stick to a spiritual routine. Waves of thoughts and emotions will always crash against the shore of our mind. But we should not let ourselves be dragged down with them.

When we strive to align with Amma through positive thoughts, loving actions and prayer, we pave our way to true contentment. We are only ever one thought away from Her. But we need to keep bringing our mind back from drifting into negativity, so that She can fill us up from within.

We are only going to receive true peace of mind when we look within and lead a good life dedicated to helping others. When we offer our life in service, not only do we heal the world around us, we heal ourselves as well.

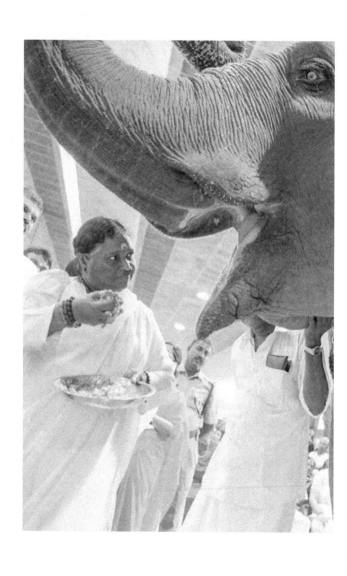

Chapter 12

Healing Trauma

*The deeper pain carves into your being,
the more joy you can contain.*

– Khalil Gibran

My daughter is not a devotee. In fact, she doesn't even like Amma, but that doesn't change the fact that Amma saved her life.

When my daughter was 16, as she was walking home from school one afternoon, a car came speeding down the street and hit her. She was thrown into the air and landed hard on the pavement. She broke her femur and suffered a host of other injuries, but she survived.

Like many people who survive life-threatening traumas, she developed an acute case of post-traumatic stress disorder. She started having panic attacks when crossing the street, became very angry and aggressive and, like many PTSD sufferers, was convinced she would die young.

After college, she went to school to study photojournalism. Her plan was to move to a country with an active conflict and take photos of the "Peace Process." The trouble with peace processes though, is that you have to find a war first.

She used to say things like, "You know, photojournalists have the highest rate of kidnappings and murders of any profession." I think she just liked to see my reaction.

In private moments, she admitted that she had no intention of living past middle age, and I don't think she had much of a desire for family life. Her plan was to travel and take pictures until she was kidnapped and killed. Not much of a plan, but I think she thought it was romantic somehow. I certainly did not.

After graduation, her first stop was India. She came to visit me in Amritapuri and also take photos of a festival in Varanasi. From there, she planned to find a war to photograph.

I admit I wasn't very nice. I was nervous about her plans and hassled her all the time. "Babies are so cute!" I would tell her. "Don't you think portraits would be a better use of your time?"

She wanted simple, pleasant, mother-daughter bonding time, but whenever we spent any time together, I would become so agitated by her bad ideas that we ended up in a fight.

The one good thing I did was pray for her incessantly. My mantra became, "Please Amma, take my daughter's heart. Please, take her heart." This prayer filled me. My daughter had never been a devotee, but in my heart, I desperately wanted Amma to claim my little girl as Her own.

Then Amma left for South India tour. I went back home to the States and my daughter stayed behind, alone in the ashram. Of course, no one in the ashram is ever really alone – Amma has made it quite clear that the ashram itself is Her body.

A few days later, something unexplainable happened: while lying on her bed one afternoon after meditating, my daughter felt a deep black, thick energy rising out of her heart, leaving her. It was as though years of trauma were just lifted away. I don't know all the details of that experience, but I know that afterwards, she was never the same.

When she came home two weeks later, her face was bright and clear – like it had been when she was a child. Not only had her acne disappeared, her face was completely relaxed, as though her pain had evaporated. People told her, "You look like you've lost ten pounds!" But it wasn't physical weight she had lost – it was emotional and spiritual.

All of a sudden we could relate in a whole new way. The fighting stopped, and it was as though we were speaking the same language for the first time in years.

Soon after, she found a journalism internship in a war zone across the world, and boarded an airplane. Every time a bomb fell, she would ask if she could go and cover the destruction. She would call me feigning disappointment; her boss kept denying her requests (he didn't think a young woman, and the most inexperienced member of the team, should be given the most dangerous assignments!).

After only six months at her dream internship, she decided to move on. It was then that I realized something had profoundly changed. Her heart wasn't in it anymore. She was distracted by her newfound love for God.

She came home and started spending a lot of time with the youth group at a local Evangelical Church. When she wasn't volunteering at the Church, she was reading the Bible or books about Jesus. She was determined to learn as much as she could about spirituality and religion. It was a complete turnaround. She had never shown even the slightest interest in God before. She had always been an artist, atheist and angry – but she was different now.

For a few months, maybe a year, my daughter did the IAM meditation on the rooftop of her church. She always wore the mala she had bought in Amritapuri. She told me she wanted to remember her miracle. But slowly, as time went on, she forgot about Amma and the mala was discarded.

All of a sudden it was "God" who had healed her. In her mind, her transformation no longer had anything to do with, "That Indian woman." As she went deeper and deeper into the Christian tradition, the less she wanted anything to do with Amma. She stopped believing in Gurus.

Today, I couldn't get her to visit Amma or an ashram, even if I pleaded. I try to tell her Amma and Jesus are the same, but she is still as stubborn as ever and doesn't want to hear it.

Thanks to Amma my daughter is very religious. She is married and lives with her husband in a safe, suburban neighbourhood. She no longer expects to be kidnapped and killed, and she doesn't have any plans to photograph in war zones. Her camera is otherwise preoccupied. It is busy taking photographs of her three beautiful children.

Amma knew when She healed my daughter's heart that she would never become a Hindu or an Amma devotee. That wasn't what was important. She is a Christ devotee, and that is more than enough.

Amma did what I could never do: She healed our child from the inside out. Whether or not Amma is ever acknowledged, thanked or praised, I am absolutely certain that She loves us completely and fully. True maternal love wants nothing more than the health and happiness of all children.

Thanks to Amma, my daughter truly has been 'Born Again.'

Amma sees the whole world as a family and sees us all as God's children. For Her there is no difference

between those who are devoted to Her form and those who are not. There are no judgments creating borders in Her mind. While we use our differences against each other, creating conflicts and wars, Amma melts away all these intangible differences into a unified stream of love.

Sometimes I feel that Amma is like a powerful MRI (magnetic resonance imaging) machine. She sees right through us, past all of our human frailties, attachments and negativities – right into the goodness that lies in each of our hearts. She knows exactly what we need, and when we come into Her embrace, she fills us up and makes us whole again. She silently lifts away the heavy burdens we have been carrying for years (or even lifetimes).

Amma never judges our beliefs, whether we are religious, spiritual or worldly people. Her only desire is for our complete healing: to make us happy if we are sad, to rejoice with us in our laughter, and to dry away the sorrow of our tears.

Chapter 13

Finding Durga Within

Out of suffering have emerged the strongest souls;
the most massive characters are seared with scars.

– Khalil Gibran

I was born in America to very loving and spiritual parents. My father had lived as a monk for seven years, and my mother was a meditation teacher. They were both very devoted to God, and they raised me with tremendous love.

I had a pure childhood full of happiness and support, but when I turned 18 all of that changed. I fell in love with a man 20 years my senior. He was magnetic and charismatic, and I thought he was very spiritual. He certainly talked about spirituality a lot. Three weeks after we met, we were married.

My parents were against the marriage and wouldn't give their approval. It was the first time in my life that I did something against their wishes, and it was the worst mistake of my life.

My husband was incredibly abusive. He forced me to discontinue contact with my friends and relatives. He regularly threatened to have me put in jail. Sometimes he threatened to kill me. He brainwashed me into believing that all our problems were my fault and constantly told me what a horrible person I was. I believed him.

I wasn't allowed to take a walk unless I had his permission. If he found out that I had spoken to anybody, either on the phone or in person, without his explicit permission, I would get a real beating that night. I lived in constant terror.

Three months after we were married, I decided to leave him. That's when I found out I was pregnant. It was the darkest day of my life. My childhood had been so beautiful, but I knew I could never pass that gift on to my child. I grappled with the decision, but in the end I chose to stay.

I started doing some small spiritual practices to lift myself up, but it was really hard. Every time I pulled myself up, he pushed me back down. Shortly after my daughter was born, my husband took us to Oklahoma, far away from everyone I knew. Anytime

I did anything that displeased him, he threatened to call the police and have them take my daughter away.

I mustered up my courage and secretly emailed my mother. She told me she had met Amma and said she would send a black and white image in the mail.

The little piece of paper that arrived was a photocopy of Amma; I taped it up on my wall. Everyday I looked at Her and cried. There was a small mantra written beneath the photo, so that mantra became my mantra. I chanted it over and over, pouring my heart out to the little photo.

When I started praying to Amma, I started to feel myself becoming stronger and stronger. One day (I don't know what came over me), I demanded that we move back home. I told my husband I was leaving Oklahoma and taking our daughter with me. He could choose to come with us or not – but we were going.

The strength I had in that moment shocked him. He relented and we moved back home. Even so, I still accepted all the horrible things he said: I believed that I was the bad one.

Once I was home, I knew how to get around. I had friends and family, and I secretly got a job. Still,

I clung tightly to that little black and white photo; it was my lifeline.

When I found out Amma was coming to America, I knew I had to meet Her. Surprising strength flowed out of me again and I insisted we go to see Her.

When we walked into the program hall, I felt I had found the whole purpose of my birth. From that moment on, all I wanted was to give my life in service.

I had already developed such an intimate relationship with Amma, through Her photo, that meeting Her face-to-face was extraordinarily powerful.

My husband and I tried to go for darshan as a family, but the people around Amma wouldn't let us. They kept separating us. When I finally went for my darshan, I was alone. It was so intense. I really felt like She already knew me; that She had been waiting for me. I was screaming on the inside: "Mother, I want freedom! I want God!" Amma held me by the shoulders and looked deep into my eyes, "OKAY!!" She said.

After darshan I could not find my husband for a long time, but it was fine. Something had shifted on the inside...I was done.

From that moment on I prayed, 'Amma, please take me. Take me now.' I didn't know how it was going to happen, but somehow I knew She was going to save me.

I became a lot more independent after that: I stopped believing my husband's mind games and torture. I moved out of our bedroom into a different room in our apartment and told my husband about my secret job. I even told him about the car I had bought (I had been hiding it down the road so he wouldn't know).

In response to my growing strength, his violence spilled out in public. Our fights started becoming so violent and loud that the neighbours began asking me if I needed help. One day the fighting escalated so violently that the moment he slammed the door to leave, a neighbour rang the bell and asked if she could take me to a woman's shelter. I thanked her but told her that it wasn't necessary. I was leaving. I packed one bag for my daughter, one for myself, and we drove away.

Amma gave me the strength to go. Praying to Her and knowing She is always there for me provided me the strength I needed to leave.

These days I have a reputation of being a superstrong woman, one who makes things happen. Amma did that for me. Before I knew Her I had been submissive, soft-spoken, and too shy to step out on a stage. I couldn't even sing in the local choir because my voice would crack from anxiety. I let my husband torture and abuse me because I was too afraid to stand up, fight back or walk away.

Amma uncovered a huge reserve of strength, courage and fearlessness within me. I had no idea it was ever there. Today I run a non-profit and give lectures all over the country. I teach classes and organise programs for hundreds of people. Thanks to Amma, I have been able to use my life to do something good.

Amma sees the priceless gems hidden within us and brings them out into the light. She cuts these gems, cultivates them, and polishes them until they begin to shine. Today I am fearless. That's the gem Amma has brought out from within me. Amma is my strength and my guiding light. She is the invincible Durga Devi within me.

When we face tremendous difficulties in life, it often seems so unfair. But no matter how many problems may come our way, we should try to survive them and strive to find some degree of equanimity in their midst. If we can do this, we will become like a lotus flower that grows tall and resilient out of the filth and mud.

We learn more from difficulties when we see them as tests we are being given to grow, to make our minds strong and pure. Amma reminds us that the strongest, finest steel is made only in the hottest furnace. Challenges and painful experiences are not given to us to punish or destroy us, but rather, to bring us to the point where we are forced to discover our true potential. Untapped treasures are concealed deep within each of us. Luckily for us, Amma sees through all of our pain and fears and helps us to discover the priceless riches we carry within us wherever we go.

With God's grace, the painful karma we need to endure can be transformed into precious life lessons. When we learn to surrender to a higher power, we become powerful, brave and receptive to our own transformation. The veil is lifted, just a little, and we are able to see the hidden beauty that lies beneath the surface.

We alone are responsible for the situations we find ourselves in; they are a result of our choices and our karma. Luckily, the Divine always gives us back what we are due in the most beautiful way: by putting us in the perfect situations that we need to grow. This can be a very painful truth to accept, but when we are able to surrender to life's situations with clarity and understanding we will gain a deep peace and ultimately transform in beautiful ways.

Be Strong. The tangled knots of karma are difficult to endure, but given time, patience, courage and correct understanding, they will unweave themselves and free us.

Chapter 14

Choosing to Live

*Faith is taking the first step, even when
you don't see the whole staircase.*

– *Martin Luther King, Jr.*

Before I met Amma, I was in and out of the hospital constantly: the Behavioural Unit for Mental Health. My only comfort in life was the thought of suicide. I don't know if I really wanted to do it, but it often seemed like my best option. A couple of times I made serious attempts on my own life, but the Divine intervened each time and I survived.

Truthfully, I didn't know what feeling 'well' meant. Whenever I had anything good, I destroyed it. I was accepted into one of the best universities in the country; I got kicked out. I couldn't hold onto a job and had to go on disability. I hated myself, and I hated life.

I couldn't even find a psychologist or psychiatrist who was willing to work with me. The therapists couldn't handle me; I was too intense for them – at least that's what they told me. Therapists routinely "fired" me.

I spent some time in jail, and even my own mother wouldn't bail me out. Since I wasn't competent to stand trial in court, my case was sent to the mental health court. From there I was sentenced to a mental hospital (again). But even in the hospital, nobody wanted me.

I went to the very best hospital in my area. I had all the right papers and the right insurance. It was my last hope. But they wouldn't even admit me. After just one look, the admitting doctor said, "Forget it. Given the circumstances, go to the State Hospital."

No one knew what to do with me, and I certainly didn't know what to do with myself. I felt completely worthless.

Truth be told, I really liked being in the hospital and I didn't want to leave. They fed me and made me take my medicines. They gave me a routine. It was more than I could do for myself.

My best friend was always worried about me. She insisted that I meet her uncle. I really didn't want to, "What's he going to do?" I argued. "He's just another horrible man." But she kept insisting.

When I finally met him, all he wanted to talk about was Amma. I kept thinking, 'Yeah, right! Some saint is going to help me. Why should I believe that?'

He kept talking, and I kept rolling my eyes. But somehow his words started getting through. What did I have to lose? There was a tiny part of me that was curious, even intrigued.

A few days later I saw a flier that said, *'Come learn about Mata Amritanandamayi.'* What were the odds of that? It was the same Amma my friend's uncle had been telling me about, so I went to the lecture. But still my guard was up, the whole thing made me suspicious.

Eventually I decided to go to Amma's local ashram, partly because I was curious, but mainly because I had nothing else to do. Amma wasn't in town at the time, but I liked the community and started going to satsang regularly.

A few months later, Amma came to the United States, and I decided I had to meet this woman. Everyone I knew was obsessed. I flew out to Seattle like all the rest of them. My friends kept asking me, "How is your first experience going? Do you like it?"

I hated it.

Smiling through clenched teeth, I lied, "Oh, it's wonderful! I love it!"

I smiled and laughed on the outside, fooling everybody except myself. My only thought was, 'I have got to get out of here. I hate this place...I want to go home!'

My friend kept pushing me to get a mantra. Every time I saw her, like a tape recorder, she just kept repeating the question, "Why don't you get a mantra?" It was all she would talk about. Reluctantly, I agreed. At least it would get her off my back.

At the end of the program, I was waiting on the balcony upstairs, ready to leave. I remember hanging over the railing, hating my life: I wanted to die. Once again, that old familiar question popped into my head, "Why don't you kill yourself?"

Out of nowhere, my mantra popped into my head and started erasing the negative thoughts, one by one. I didn't even know how to say the mantra properly, but there it was, repeating itself over and over in my mind. I could feel Amma's presence beside me, supporting me.

When I went home, I immersed myself in seva. Although my mind was telling me that I hated everything about Amma, somehow there was a pull that I couldn't resist. I found myself doing hours and hours of seva helping to prepare for Amma's visit to our city. For weeks I was totally immersed in spiritual practice, doing seva and chanting my mantra over and over again. Don't get me wrong, the depression was still hanging over me, and I still couldn't figure out what I was doing or why. But nonetheless, I felt an irresistible draw towards seva and mantra japa.

Slowly my hatred and anger started melting away.

Several years (and countless meltdowns) later, a devotee dragged me up to Amma – literally dragged me. She held me tightly by the arm and hauled me right up next to Her chair. I did not want to be there, but she refused to let go until she had pushed me down in the spot right next to Amma.

They spoke for a few minutes, and Amma said to me through a translator, "You have to listen to the doctors and stay on medication. If not, the police will come and take you away." That was all She had to say.

I didn't trust the medicines. When I wasn't in the hospital or ordered by the court to take them, my meds would always find their way into the trash (despite the doctor's orders). But as soon as Amma said the word 'police,' I knew I had to listen. I was terrified at the idea of going back to jail.

At the end of the program as Amma was getting into Her car, I called out, "Amma, Amma…I want to ride in the RV with you." I didn't know if She could hear me. "AMMA!" I yelled. Everyone stared.

Amma turned around.

She looked at me with those eyes…eyes that said, 'Uh huh. You want to ride in the RV with me?' Then She looked at me straight, eye-to-eye, and stated very seriously, "Take tablet. Take tablet!"

As soon as I got home, I called the doctors and said something I never thought I would say in my life: "I need medication! Get me some medication! I need it *now*!"

Through Amma's influence, slowly my life has transformed. Today I am working with the most amazing therapist. She can handle me even on my most difficult days – she's a devotee, and Amma is the foundation of our relationship. I've started school again, and I am starting to get my life together for the first time.

I remember at the very first program I attended in Seattle, Amma said, "Pray for grace, even if you do not feel it. Always remember that God and Guru will take care of you, no matter how you feel." I didn't fully trust Her at the time. Despite that, I found myself praying for Her grace over and over again – praying for Her to look out for me and to take care of me. I can't explain it. Maybe I was desperate...Nothing else worked, but that did.

In the past, I was filled with so much anger and hatred towards myself. But today I've learned to trust. I know Amma is always with me, and I know She is never going to leave me alone. She loves me, and She takes care of me.

Only when you strip away all of the labels can you see Amma for who She truly is: pure love and pure compassion. When you don't know what love and compassion are, they can be very difficult to receive. Trust me, I know.

Before I met Amma, I was completely lost, broken and alone. I had no one and I wanted to take my own life. Amma changed everything.

I still have bad days, lots of them, but for the first time, I know I'm okay. For years my only comfort was the thought of suicide. Now, it's not even an option anymore. Amma is teaching me to live.

All too often we live imprisoned, stuck in a closed off world we have created for ourselves. We want to blame our external surroundings, other people, or even God for our troubles, but in truth, it is our own past actions and inner attitude that has landed us where we are.

We end up trapped in a sticky web, woven from the repetition of our own bad habits. When we are stuck like this, it seems almost impossible to release ourselves. Yet, Amma holds the secret solution that can dissolve the web, untie our knots…and free us.

Whatever our circumstances, we all experience the world totally differently. Most of us base our decisions and judgments on our frequently changing thoughts and emotions. These are always passing through us and keep us from being able to see reality clearly. But that is not the way Amma lives Her life; Her vision is always clear.

Someone who has obtained the pure state of God-realization is free from the turmoil of incessantly churning thoughts and emotions. *Clarity and clear vision spontaneously flow through them, directly from an inner wisdom. They remain continually connected to the Divine.*

Amma says the only way the world can heal itself is through the power of love. And that is why She is here in this form. Amma's love is here for us all the time... we just need to remember that Her love is only ever a thought away. Amma's presence is God's greatest gift to our suffering world.

Chapter 15

Choosing Light

*Nothing is softer or more flexible than
water, yet nothing can resist it.*

– Lao Tzu

I arrived in Amritapuri on Christmas Day, 2007 at
1:30 a.m. I was given a room in the temple and went
to bed at 2 a.m. I had never met Amma before, but
that night I dreamt that I received Her darshan. It
was so vivid. She welcomed me and connected Her
heart to mine. She gave me some advice, which I
still remember, and then, while She was holding
me, I woke up.

It was 5 a.m. Archana, the chanting of the 1000
names of the Divine Mother, had begun. Mantras
resounded throughout the ashram. I could hear the
men chanting in the darshan hall and the women
in the temple. I jumped out of bed and ran down
the stairs.

It was Christmas Day in Amritapuri, and I felt just like a kid in a playground. The whole place seemed enchanted. I had only slept three hours, but I was full of energy and excitement. I received my very first darshan, and it truly was the most magical Christmas of my life.

That night I couldn't sleep. I was wide-awake and still exploring the ashram at 3 a.m. As I walked towards the stage (even though it was all walled off), I could hear music, so I opened the door to see what was going on. There was Amma, practicing bhajans, surrounded by about 20 people.

I joined in on this very intimate bhajan scene. Amma sang the same song over and over again. It sounded like a lullaby. I started to drift off to sleep when a very sharp tap on my shoulder roused me. Everyone in the room was staring at me, including the Divine Mother Herself. Looking right into my eyes, Amma said forcefully, "Wake up my son, wake up." The significance of Her words was not lost on me.

Before I met Amma I had everything I wanted: a pretty girlfriend, a condo, a car, a leather couch, HD TV. I liked my job. I lived in a beautiful city and I had a great dog. I chased my desires, occasionally used drugs, and sought out what I thought was happiness. I had all the comforts, but none of the satisfaction I was looking for deep down.

I went back to the west after that Christmas and resumed my life where it had left off. I continued to grow closer to Amma, visited Her when I could, and started doing some spiritual practices (occasionally), but nothing else really changed.

A few years later, Amma came back again in a dream. In one hand She was holding me. I was standing next to my girlfriend and we had a child. In the other hand, I was sitting in full lotus meditation in Her palm, entirely surround by light. She looked at me and said, "CHOOSE." The power of Her words woke me up.

The message was clear: do you want a family life with the white picket fence, or do you want to be surrounded by divine light? I left my girlfriend, sold my condo and moved to India.

The years since have been the most incredible of my life – being with Amma, touring with Her, associating with people who are full of devotion. I feel connected to my real Self, to who I really am, beyond the ego.

I have always been a joyful person, a pleasure seeker, but in the past, my happiness was always based on external things: the giant TV, the flashy car, the beautiful girl. Now I feel this deep joy inside myself, it is always there. It is a presence, a deep satisfaction that doesn't require me to seek anything other than what's already inside.

Most people don't know how to find true happiness. Like them, I looked for happiness in external situations, but in the end, it always left me feeling empty, sad, and unsatisfied with life. I wasn't happy with who I was.

Now my whole life has become the 'Prasad of the Guru.' Whatever I go through, the ups and the downs, it all feels like a gift. For the first time, I am comfortable in aloneness. I am no longer seeking anything other than God. She's the One I was yearning for all along,

I feel that it is entirely God's grace that I exist. I am grateful to wake up every day. For the first time in my life, I am completely content. It is amazing to feel like this – to be joyful simply because I am alive.

When Amma sees devotees who genuinely under-stand the drawbacks of materialism, Her eyes light up with pride. She says, "My children have broken their shackles. They simply desire to work selflessly for the sake of others, because of this, they will gain the greatest wealth imaginable: peace of mind."

It is thrilling to think that one actually can over-come the temptations of maya (illusion). Maya attracts us so sweetly with material luxuries, name and fame, but when we give in to her temptations; she viciously turns on us and shackles us in chains of misery.

It is important to do your dharma and be responsi-ble for your work and your family, but always remem-ber that these things can never make you permanently happy. Society pressures young people to get married and have children, making them believe that their lives are going to be perfect after that. But when couples lack maturity and patience, they fight, become miserable and separate, breaking their families apart.

Children then grow up to repeat the same dysfunc-tional behaviours they learned from their parents. The cycle goes on and on. The perfect dream we are seeking does not exist in the world.

It doesn't matter whether we choose an ashram life or a family life, for both, the truth is the same: only a

131

life rooted in a good value system will bring the content-ment we are longing for. Only when we learn to live by higher principles can we experience true fulfillment.

Chapter 16

True Yoga

The wound is the place where the light enters you.

– Rumi

I was standing on my balcony, smoking a cigarette, when suddenly the balcony collapsed underneath me. In an instant, my life literally dropped out from under me.

I had been very successful. I was a single mom and had earned a very comfortable level of financial security. My life felt full of purpose and grace, yet I had an aversion to spiritual practices and teachings.

Then, in an instant, I found myself in the orthopedic ward of a hospital with a doctor standing at my bedside showing me a whole host of x-rays: a pelvis fractured in multiple places, a fractured sacrum, several spinal cord injuries. My hands were broken; my feet were broken. My perfect life was broken.

A broken back is a broken back – no matter how many doctors' opinions you get. I had a rare, very painful, sacral spinal cord injury. It was so severe that if someone even lightly touched the edge of my bed, my whole body would convulse in spasms.

Before the accident, I remained aloof, removed from other people. After all, I was the strategic advisor for a big, important company; but in an instant this high flyer had crash-landed into reality.

Just to survive, I had to force open my heart to all the nurses and hospital staff. No amount of money was going to make them care whether they hurt me or not. No amount of strategy was going to land me a better nurse.

My recovery felt hopeless. Nothing the doctors were doing was helping the pain, and nothing they were doing was helping me to move.

Eventually, I realized that I could move slightly if I remained very still, quiet, and detached. The only way to do this was to change the rhythm of my breath. If I slowed my breath, I could slow my body and reduce the pain.

When I remained in awareness and directed my breath, my body responded. I made up a few little breathing practices of my own. When I used them,

I could feel my toes. When my concentration, that dharana (one-pointedness) was broken, the pain would come rushing back.

Having no intention of living in a hospital bed or being bound to a wheelchair for the rest of my life, I started to do the practices I invented several times a day. The results were remarkable; I started to heal incredibly quickly.

The more the staff saw my dedication, the more they tried to help me. When people in the ward saw that my practices were working, they asked, "Hey, what are you doing? Can we do what you're doing?" Soon the entire ward was busy breathing and moving our bodies. We were learning how to heal ourselves.

There was a woman in the ward, a very beautiful black woman from a lower-middle class family. She had a back brace on. Her family, including all her little children, visited every day. This was South Africa; because of our country's history and political background, I was especially aware of her suffering. A truck had hit her at work, and she had just had her fourth spinal operation to correct the damage. The family had gone into major debt.

The nurses seemed to be indifferent towards her, but I couldn't figure out why. When I asked, they told me they had overheard her family agreeing that it was better for her to ignore the doctor's instructions and intentionally paralyze herself – because only then would the state insurance kick in.

I was horrified that in a developed country, in a state-of-the-art hospital, a woman was deliberately choosing to become paralyzed to avoid being financially destroyed by medical bills.

At that moment, I decided I would help people in her situation. I couldn't help right then because both my hands were still broken, but I was determined to do something. I was released from the hospital a month later. I still wasn't walking properly and had to rest a lot, but I managed to get onto crutches. I also continued to carry on with the practices I had been doing in my hospital bed.

During these practices, I would quietly listen to my body and do (what I later learned were) yoga asanas. I even used to slide to the edge of my bed to do a shoulder stand. I didn't know this was yoga, I only knew that the practices helped.

I tried every massage therapist, every so-called 'healer' I could find, but the minute I began the litany of my injuries: "My pelvis is broken in five places, my sacrum is fractured, my elbow is…" They would say, "Please phone us back in a year."

Only then, did I realize how painstakingly difficult it is to find anyone who is willing to help those most in need. To massage a paraplegic or someone having chemo, rather than a housewife who has a little crick in her neck, takes a rare amount of courage.

After phoning 64 different healers, I finally found a paramedic who agreed to come and give me massages every three days. He even brought an inversion table for me to borrow.

I started a whole regime of inversion practices, synchronizing them with the breathing and movement practices I had been doing before. Within six months, I started walking, driving and was even able to take airplanes again. Even so, if I lost awareness for even the shortest time, the pain returned.

When I finally felt well enough, I decided to go for a haircut (I had been putting it off because it hurt to sit for too long). The hairdresser gave me a card that read: 'YOGA.' I thought, 'How difficult can that be?' I grinned as I imagined a whole lot of hippies dancing around. I figured it couldn't do any harm.

The teacher on the phone laughed when I told her of all my injuries, "No, you can't come to my class, but there is a remedial yoga therapy teacher in an ashram nearby."

That remedial yoga class became my new home. When I explained my body-awareness and breathing practices, the teacher said excitedly, "Oh, that IS yoga! You have been doing yoga all of this time!" I went to class three times a week for two years, and it gave me the strength to accept my transformation.

When I was healed, I decided to sell everything I owned and use the money to start a charity organization. It would be an Ayurveda and yoga therapy program for those with major disabilities and injuries. I named it 'Brave.'

I wanted Brave to be a place where anyone could come, where people could give a small donation or nothing at all, and money would make no difference. At Brave, a lack of finances would not prevent the healing process.

Then one of Amma's devotees arrived in South Africa and gave a satsang (spiritual talk) to my community. We watched the "Embracing The World" video. To be honest, I don't really remember the darshan part. I was completely mesmerized by the vast number of charities that Amma runs. After watching the video, I thought, 'Okay! This is it! If

Amma can run all of these charities, then I can run one little organization!' I felt completely inspired.

Right around the time I was forming Brave, my son was finishing high school. As a graduation gift, I told him I would take him to India. I wanted to meet Amma and see what I could learn about running my organization.

We arrived in Amritapuri...and there was Amma. I didn't quite know how to process it.

I had no expectations about Amma's darshan the first time I went to see Her. I was just there to learn how to help people. But when I looked up and saw Amma giving darshan for the first time, a wave of absolute sorrow and pain washed over me – I could feel each of those thousands of people's pain. I burst into tears and could not stop crying.

We bought garlands and joined the darshan queue. As the queue edged closer and closer to Amma, the pain I had been feeling started to transform into light, into bliss. It was heavenly.

When I was finally in front of Amma, I couldn't speak. Instead, I asked Her mentally, 'Help me to help those who are suffering.' As my son and I walked off the stage, a brahmachari who was standing there asked me, "Are you the remedial yoga therapy teacher?" I hadn't said a word about my work to anyone. "Please come with me, there is someone with Parkinson's who needs you."

A few days later, I felt I should go on a pilgrimage to visit the headquarters of my Yoga Centre, so off we went. We arrived and settled in. During that first night, I had a powerful dream. I heard the booming laughter of the Swami who had founded my Yoga School (he had passed away many years before). Then I heard Amma laughing too. I saw their two faces looking at me together, side-by-side. Swami said, "Look at you! What are you doing looking for me here in a statue, when I am alive in Amma?"

I didn't even wait for the sun to come up. I grabbed my son, and we rushed back to Amritapuri. I realized then that Divine light isn't exclusive to any one form or situation. The Divine is in everything.

At my healing centre, we have people from various religions, races and economic backgrounds. Our patients come with different types of injuries and illnesses, and we help each other to heal. Despite all the differences, we are one family. It is a melting pot – just like Amma's ashram. So even though we have beautiful pictures of Amma everywhere, families from every faith allow their children to sit and chant AUM together.

When I visited the Ashram recently, I brought a large, framed photograph to offer to Amma. In the image, my patients are holding a photo of Amma next to a photo of Nelson Mandela. Amma loved it. I feel that this photo so aptly represents the times we are living in now. There is so much pain, but at the same time, we are being showered with tremendous grace.

Love and service truly are the highest forms of sadhana. They are the greatest actions we can ever perform. Amma is healing the pain of the world, everyday. She is inspiring us to use our gifts in service instead of dwelling in our own pain and suffering. Helping another is really the best way we can help ourselves. Amma is trying to inspire each of us to do our part, in whatever simple way we can.

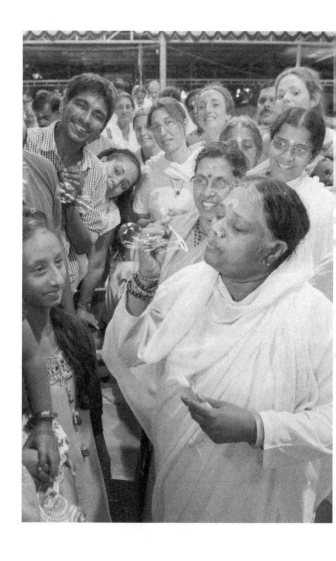

Chapter 17

The Vasana Box

*All that I am, or hope to be, I
owe to my angel mother.*

– *Abraham Lincoln*

I was feeling really low one summer. My negativities
seemed completely overwhelming. Usually when I
get too negative, I stay away from Amma; the more
negative I get, the further away I stay. I know that
negativity is only distance from God, but when I am
in that distant place, I feel so repulsive and disgust-
ing. I think to myself, 'How can I go near something
so radiant and beautiful?' Not that I could taint it,
but it's just too embarrassing.

After much inner turmoil, I finally persuaded
myself to bring a question up to Amma, hoping that
She would transform me. I wrote my question out
on a little square of paper: *'When I am overcome with
negativity, should I find someone to unburden myself*

*to? I am shy to come to Amma because everyone will
overhear everything.'*

She pulled my ear and smiled at me sweetly.
"Everyone has this problem. Don't worry. Unburden
yourself to Amma." She quoted a bhajan that says
that we must peel ourselves away before the Guru
just like we peel away the layers of an onion: "Let
me give you my shame, my jealousy..."

Inspired by Amma's words, I wanted to offer all
of myself to Amma: the good and the bad. I knew I
needed to admit my helplessness and powerlessness.
I wanted to tell Her: "I can't do this alone. I need
your grace."

I found a beautiful little box...

I decided to put all of my vasanas (negative ten-
dencies) into the box. I found colourful scraps of
material and wrote out all of my different vasanas:
fear, laziness, anger, depression and greed. I could
have gone on, but I thought it best to keep it simple.
I didn't want to be too descriptive!

I found a clear plastic bag, put the vasanas into
the bag and wrote 'Trash' on the outside. I also put
a small jewelry container into the box. On the top
of that I wrote 'Wealth,' to symbolize my virtuous

qualities. But I couldn't think of anything to put in there, so I left it empty.

I wrote everything in Malayalam so that Amma could read it directly. This way I could have the privacy I wanted. I wouldn't need a translator, and nobody but Amma would see it.

My prayer was simple, and I repeated it over and over as I prepared for darshan: 'Please Amma, take out the trash.'

I turned the box towards Amma and said in Malayalam (as best I could), "Amma, this is a vasana box!" One by one, She read each vasana aloud and then carefully put each little paper back inside the box. Then She pulled them all back out, and re-read each vasana (loudly) all over again. "You forgot some," She mused. "Jealousy, rivalry and lust!"

When She got to the wealth box, She opened it and said, "Oh, poor thing!" and laughed. She gave the box back to me. 'Well, at least they are blessed,' I sighed to myself. I had been hoping She would keep them.

That night we flew back to India. Amma sat with us as we waited in the airport terminal. I sat a little towards the back. Suddenly She turned and looked right at me. She gave me a beautiful smile, the most beautiful smile I've ever seen. She seemed so pleased with me – so happy – and She started talking about the vasana box.

"This boy gave me a vasana box!" She announced loudly. She repeated every single vasana I had written out for Her. She laughed, "There was a wealth box too, but it was empty."

I was star struck. As if in a trance I got up, stepping over (or perhaps on top of) six or seven people, to get close to Amma. I settled down right at Her feet (half-sitting on someone's lap). "Do you have it?" Amma asked. "I want to see it!"

I told Her that I had put the box in my check-in luggage, but would give it to Her as soon as we arrived in Amritapuri.

I added in the extra vasanas Amma had mentioned and brought the box to Her room. When I gave it to Her attendant, I didn't expect Amma to actually look at it again (as people give Amma many things every day), but I felt a huge sense of relief – as though I had given my vasanas to God. 'Okay, it's finished,' I told myself.

But it wasn't over. That night, when Amma came for bhajans, I could see She was holding something unusual in Her hands, but I couldn't quite make out what it was. I strained to see. 'No. It's not possible,' I thought. 'It can't be…' but there She was, holding my vasana box in front of the entire ashram – thousands of people!

Amma called out into the microphone, "Whose box is this?" I wanted to hide under the table, but I timidly raised my hand.

She told the whole Ashram, "This is a vasana box. That boy gave me a vasana box!" All eyes turned towards me as She read each one of my vasanas into the microphone.

After bhajans I ran to wait for Amma outside of Her room, just in case She wanted to talk to me. She stopped and looked at me. Then She told everyone around us excitedly, "This is the boy who gave me the vasana box! He gave me a box full of vasanas!"

The next day, during darshan, I had to go to the stage to ask someone a question about my seva. Amma spotted me and called me over. She was just as excited as She had been the day before: "Oh! This is the boy who gave me the vasana box!" She told everyone around Her all about my vasana box and meticulously listed each of the vasanas inside.

I had at least six interactions with Amma about that box, and each conversation drew me closer to Her.

But it didn't end there. The vasana box had become a celebrity. It was featured in the ashram scripture class, in an article and photo on Amma's website, it starred on Amma's Facebook page and in an article in Matruvani magazine. The irony, of course, is that this whole thing started because I was too shy to go up to Amma – I didn't want anyone to know my issues!

I can't quite describe the feeling I had when I saw Amma holding the box…it was thrilling, so intimate. It felt like I was Amma's show-and-tell that day: as though She had brought me to school with Her and proudly showed me off to all the kids in Her class.

The best part was how funny She made the whole thing. All too often I feel like an enormous calamity: a great, big, horrible tragedy. But in Her gracious, down-to-earth way, She took all of my fears, all of my negativities and turned them into a great, big joke. With Her warm humour, She took my shame away.

*Dealing with our vasanas can be extremely diffi-
cult. Sometimes, no matter how hard we try we can't
seem to change. But when we learn to go beyond our
shame and surrender our negativities at the feet of the
Guru, our subtle vasanas can start to be wiped away.
It takes an awful lot of self-effort and perseverance to
be able to do this.*

*We all have faults and bad habits, but this fact
should not disable us. Amma says, "You can never make
friends with the mind. It will always be your enemy. It
will always try to drag you down. Try to take charge of
your thoughts, even if you have to pretend."*

*We waste so much time imagining negative things.
Instead, we should use our imagination in a positive
way, pretending something good is going to happen
(but be careful to keep your expectations in check!). A
single positive thought has the potential to pull us out
of the negative spheres that we often get dragged into.*

*A few years back, while we were traveling on an
Indian tour, a young man who had just met Amma
joined the pilgrimage. One of the highlights of Indian
tours is Amma serving prasad dinner. 'Seconds' are
always passed around for those who are still hungry.*

The correct etiquette is to take one or two chapattis (or whatever food is being passed around), and then to pass the rest on to share with everyone else.

But when the 'seconds' plate, with the enormous pile of chapattis came to this young man, he thought it was all for him! So he ate something like forty chapattis that night! He ate and ate until he was too full to even move.

Amma carefully watched him eat, and when he was finished She called him over. She told him that in the Vedic scriptures there is a demon called 'Bagan.' This demon was so ravenous that he used to devour entire villages: cows, dogs, and even humans. Amma said She never used to believe the stories were true – until She met him. Now She knew it was possible! Everyone laughed, especially him.

He told me afterwards that he was completely blissed out by the experience. He felt like a small puppy, basking in Amma's gentle teasing. In that moment he felt completely loved, seen and accepted by Her and the community around Her.

Everyone has desires; it is nothing to be ashamed of. But when we decide it is time to pursue a higher goal, then our constant desires will begin to loosen their grip on us. When we decide to make the conscious effort to move in a positive direction, a flow of grace is unleashed.

When we make even just a little effort to control the negativities that box us in, and try to do the right thing, Amma's grace will surely pick us up and carry us the rest of the way.

Chapter 18

Finding Peace

*"Dance, when you're broken open. Dance,
if you've torn the bandage off. Dance in
the middle of the fighting. Dance in your
blood. Dance when you're perfectly free."*

— Rumi

Before I met Amma, I lived for the thrill. I was always craving that ultimate rush…when you feel more alive than you have ever felt, when your heart is beating as hard as it can possibly beat…when your blood is pumping as fast as it can go – *that feeling of being completely alive.*

I didn't care about anyone or anything else. My life was entirely centred on the rush, the thrill: life on the extreme edge. I didn't sleep for three days after skydiving, because I was so high. When I surfed 15-foot waves, I felt like I was God, walking on water. When I went rock climbing, I realized just how high I truly was.

I used to go surfing, skydiving and rock-climbing all on drugs. I kid you not. Some days I wouldn't even know if I was sober or not when I went out for the extreme sports.

I worked two nights a week, Friday and Saturday, at a local bar. I was a specialty bartender and made a ton of money. I did stunts, played with fire. I would splash alcohol on the counter and literally set the bar on fire. That was my 'day-job,' the rest of my time was devoted to seeking the ultimate rush.

I'd wake up at noon, drink a coffee, smoke a joint, pick up the phone and dial my best friend. "Hey Bro, what are we doing today…?"

I wasn't a good person, and spirituality was the farthest thing from my mind. I lived on the dark side of life and had no intention of ever growing up.

Then I met my wife.

When we started dating, I visited her parent's house. The first thing I noticed was a photo hanging on the wall – a photo of bare feet – an Indian woman's feet.

Her family had no furniture in their living room. Instead, they had pillows lying all over the floor. I thought, 'Oh no, what did I get myself into with this girl?' But at the same time, I was completely fascinated by those feet. I asked my girlfriend whose feet they were, what that lady was all about, and (most importantly), why they had no furniture!

At first she was hesitant to tell me about Amma, but eventually she gave in. She invited me to satsang at their house, and I went that weekend. When I got there, the room was packed. Everybody was crammed in and sitting on the pillows scattered all over the floor.

Her stepdad played the drums (tablas, actually) and her mom played the keyboard (it was a harmonium, but I didn't know that at the time). They sang Indian songs, but I couldn't sing because I couldn't figure out how to read the words. When I think back, I realize how long ago that was and how much is different for me now.

They did arati that evening, waving the burning camphor around the photo of Amma. I thought it was funny when the smoke alarm went off.

Later that week, I asked my girlfriend if I could meet Amma.

We found cheap plane tickets and arrived at Amma's program in Toronto several weeks later.

There were so many people – people everywhere. Everyone was waiting to get a hug from Amma. I thought, 'Wow, this woman certainly won't be able to give everyone a hug today.' It was Devi Bhava, and of course She did.

Someone asked me if I would like to do seva. I didn't even know what the word meant, but I thought, 'Okay, I'll help. Why not?' He asked me to pass out the holy water Amma had blessed. Being a bartender, I thought, 'I can carry a tray of water. No problem.' I didn't realize the tray was covered with dozens of tiny cups, each one filled to the brim with holy water – and there were no lids.

The guy in charge asked me to carry the tray to the people sitting outside. I walked outside, and my jaw dropped. There were thousands upon thousands of people waiting outside in the parking lot. They were all watching Amma live on really big screens.

I was stampeded. As soon as it became known that I was holding a tray of holy water, hundreds of people rushed towards me. I went back and forth for about an hour giving out water to every single person.

While waiting for Amma's darshan, I explored the scene. Finally (after about nine hours!) my token number was called. I walked onto the stage and kneeled in front of Her. She smiled and pulled me in. I didn't understand what She said, but She spoke in my ear and gave me two chocolate kisses and a rose petal. As I stood up I asked the translator what Amma had said. He replied, "Amma says you need a mantra."

I didn't know what a mantra was, but I immediately trusted Her. She told me to sit beside Her. I sat there for two hours.

When She whispered the mantra into my ear, that's when my soul really began to transform.

It's been a slow process, and it has taken years, but every time I see Amma, something else shifts: my morals, my values, everything has changed. I became a person with a purpose, a person who wants to live for something, to help other people, to make a difference in the world. (I even do dishes sometimes.)

Before I met Amma, I used to wake up in the morning, and my first thought would be *'I need to go skydiving!'* I had no responsibilities, and I didn't care about anyone.

These days when I wake up, my first thought is 'Amma...' I still seek the thrill and the rush, but now I get it from Her. My excitement comes from watching Amma give darshan, from meditating, from doing seva. I don't need any other thrill or high. My life is finally full. I am more alive today than I have ever been.

Flash forward ten years: I am married, we have a son and I run my own business. I never could have imagined that would be my life. None of it would have been possible without Her.

Amma transformed me.

Every Sunday since that very first darshan, I've been volunteering at a homeless shelter. It's my version of going to church, my way of expressing gratitude to Amma and giving back a little. We make sandwiches, soups and desserts. I always bring my son with me – he's been doing seva ever since he was a baby. I'm teaching him good values: to love and care about others – to serve.

Sometimes my friend comes too…the one I used to call every morning for 20 years. He stands on line with all the other homeless, shivering in the cold, waiting for his one hot meal. I always smile sadly when I see him. "Hey Bro…" I say, "Here's your sandwich." It's the one way I can help him.

He lost everything to find that thrill: his wife, his family, his home.

Me? I've found the ultimate thrill, and She saved me.

Amma's mere touch holds the power to launch us on a profound healing journey. By virtue of Her compassion and people's sincere faith, Amma is able to act as a catalyst, allowing remarkable stories of transformation to spring up all around Her.

Amma pulls us close to Her Self in innumerable ways. She softens our hearts and reminds us how to be truly human. Through Her grace, wisdom and infinite patience, She helps us to slowly remember Her teaching: that we are all embodiments of pure love and the Supreme Consciousness.

There is a story Amma often tells about two disciples: the two men travel to a village to buy fruit and vegetables for their Guru. When they come back, both are sporting bruises. Concerned, the Guru asks, "What happened?"

One of the men points at the other and replies, "He called me a monkey!"

The Guru sighs, "I have been telling you for over 20 years that you are embodiments of Supreme Consciousness, but despite all my best efforts, you never believe me. Then, just once, he calls you a monkey – and look what happens!"

All too often we behave like the men in this story. We have the entire creation inside of ourselves, but instead of radiating Divine light, we hide away in our own shadow.

Amma carries us out of the shadows, guiding us from darkness into light. She ignites the spark of love inside our heart. Amma provides hope when we are stuck in despair and provides light when darkness consumes our vision. She heals the incurable and mends the broken. With Amma's grace, the impossible becomes possible, and ordinary life is transformed into love.

All too often we search for happiness outside of ourselves, forgetting that the true source of contentment lies within. We can only find Divine luminescence on the inside, not in the bright, shiny lights of the world. When positive energy is flowing within, we find the strength to face anything.

A few years ago, someone told me a story about Rishi, Amma's little puppy. One day he went to the cowshed looking for a playmate. The cows, well...they weren't in a playful mood. This often happened to Rishi; nobody wanted to play with him.

Rishi flopped around playfully in the shed, clearly bothering all of the cows – some of them merely looked at him warily, while one or two looked ready to charge him. Rishi, in his enthusiastic innocence, thought it was a game! His response (if a dog could talk) was something like, "My God! This is so much fun!! My aunties and sisters all want to play with me!"

He rushed over, barking at them, trying to get near enough to nip at their feet a little bit. The cows had had enough. They charged him. Rishi was oblivious to their mood. He was in such ecstasy, having discovered the most fun new game you could ever imagine.

We should all strive to be Rishis, to go through life with that kind of innocence. We get to choose: we can be like Rishi, or we can be like the grumpy cows. Don't worry about what everyone else is thinking; do what you know is right. Despite external circumstances, choose to see the world as a beautiful play.

Even if those around you don't want to see the world as a magnificent Divine play, that's okay. If you hold onto an attitude of awe and wonder, you will be able to be fully joyful in the present moment. That's all what we have to do: keep the light all around us, wherever we go. Shine and be happy.

CPSIA information can be obtained
at www.ICGtesting.com
Printed in the USA
BVHW04s1335210718
522051BV00001B/185/P